"This is a guidebook that really *guides,* setting students on their path towards their journey to the future. Chapter after chapter offers practical exercises and career planning resources. It's self-directed learning at its best."

—Donna M. Bourassa, Director of Student Life
Bennington College

"This book speaks to all different types of students with all kinds of different experiences and needs. Before I read it, I thought I knew everything there was to know about making a successful transition. I learned a lot of new things! The section on graduate and professional schools helped me focus my professional goals and aspirations while in graduate school. Every chapter is full of useful information."

—Kurt Enger
Goucher College, 1995,
Harvard Graduate School of Education, 1996

"If I could, I would make Carol Weinberg's *A Transition Guide for College Juniors and Seniors* required reading for every student at my university. There is so much useful, sensible, up-to-date information written with the perspective and language of a college student, but with the wisdom of someone who has been there and done her homework. Thought-provoking exercises ask all the right questions to help guide the reader's path as they cross the transitional bridge to life after college. Professor Weinberg makes the anticipated new situation sound exciting, fun, and adventurous instead of intimidating and terrifying. Getting a job or gaining admission to graduate school are important, but this book will make whatever life the new graduate chooses easier and better."

—Arden Showalter
Director, Career Center
Southern Methodist University

CAROL WEINBERG

THE TRANSITION GUIDE

FOR COLLEGE JUNIORS AND SENIORS

How to Prepare for the Future

NEW YORK UNIVERSITY PRESS
New York and London

Quotation from *Dave Barry Talks Back,* copyright © 1991 by Dave Barry, reprinted by permission of Crown Publishers; quotation from *Dave Barry's Bad Habits,* copyright © 1987, Henry Holt and Company, Inc., reprinted by permission of Crown Publishers; quotation from *Fatherhood,* copyright © 1986 by William H. Cosby, Jr., reprinted by permission of Doubleday Publishing; quotation from "Eating Our Medicine" in *Value Judgments* by Ellen Goodman, copyright © 1993, The Boston Globe Newspaper Co./Washington Post Writers Group, reprinted with permission; quotation from *The Women of Brewster Place,* by Gloria Naylor, copyright © 1980, 1982 by Gloria Naylor, used by permission of Viking Penguin, a division of Penguin Books USA Inc.; quotations from *Naked Beneath My Clothes* by Rita Rudner, copyright © 1992 by Rita Rudner Enterprises, Inc., illustrations copyright © 1992 by Mike Lester, used by permission of Viking Penguin, a division of Penguin Books USA, Inc.; quotation from *The Search for Signs of Intelligent Life in the Universe,* copyright © 1986 by Jane Wagner Inc., reprinted by permission of HarperCollins Publishers Inc.; quotation from "Uncommon Women and Others" in *The Heidi Chronicles and Other Plays,* copyright © 1978 by Wendy Wasserstein, reprinted by permission of Harcourt Brace and Company; quotation from *Fences,* by August Wilson, copyright © 1986 by August Wilson, used by permission of Dutton Signet, a division of Penguin Books USA Inc.

Library of Congress Cataloging-in-Publication Data
Weinberg, Carol.
The transition guide for college juniors and seniors : how to
prepare for the future / Carol Weinberg.
  p.   cm.
Includes bibliographical references (p.   ) and index.
ISBN 0-8147-9285-5 (cloth).—ISBN 0-8147-9306-1 (paper)
1. School-to-work transition—United States.   2. College students—
Employment—United States   3. College students—United States—
Finance, Personal.   4. Student affairs services—United States.
5. Counseling in higher education—United States.   I. Title.
LB2342.9.W45   1996
378.1'94'25—dc20   96-17615   CIP

To

Al
Carl
Sandy
Stu
Susie
Vicki

who have been there for me through many transitions.

There is no one real world. There is the world that each of you will create for yourselves and for each other, and college will be a reference point forever.

— Andrew Bergman, writer and film director, in a commencement address to Binghamton University's graduating class of 1994.

CONTENTS

ACKNOWLEDGMENTS

I'm grateful to the college graduates who shared their own experiences with me and contributed to this book: Peter Angritt, Kieran Ayre, Susan Brown, Tiffany Burton, David Calkins, Tina Caretti, Vicki Cohen, Cami Colarossi, Karole Delaney, Jennifer Dyer, Jane Floyd, Jennifer Granducci, Mary Hoey, Ann Jackson Hutson, Christina Kay, Marian Mankin, Peter Margulis, Susie Margulis, Lisa Mix, Edward Morgereth, Jason Morton, Mogy Omatete, Toju Omatete, Joely Parker, Jenifer Reed, Caroline Ren, Sara Sclaroff, Allison Vermillion, and Melford Weiss.

Thanks also to the professionals who provided much information from their perspectives: Richard Aarons, Baltimore County Chamber of Commerce; Cornelius Bull, president of the Center for Interim Programs; Alene Crenson, Baltimore County Public Library; Sheryl Davis, president of DAQ Associates Inc., T/A Uniforce Services Inc.; LeRoy Haile, Jr., president of LeRoy Y. Haile Real Estate; U.S. Army Sergeant First Class Richard Klinger; Melvin Kryglik, agent and broker for Nationwide Insurance Company; Peter Margulis, M.D., psychiatrist with Rush Prudential HMO; Carol Paull, customer service manager of NationsBank; June Risley, financial advisor; Betsy Sapp, real estate agent; and Sara

Sclaroff, technical recruiter for United States Fidelity and Guarantee Insurance Company.

Many of my colleagues at Goucher College also contributed to this project: Larry Bielawski, Helen Schlossberg Cohen, George Delahunty, Edward Duggan, Laurie Kaplan, Jean Nair, Carolyn North, Faye Perry, Rev. Bill Rich, and Lee Stevens.

I especially want to acknowledge the help of four individuals who not only provided information, but also reviewed specific chapters and gave me much appreciated feedback: Tina Caretti, career counselor at Goucher College; Maggie Whall, nurse practitioner in private practice; Stuart Weinberg, certified public accountant with Blumer and Weinberg C.P.A.; and Marianne Leedy, financial advisor with Gardner Montgomery and Company. Thanks also to my sister, Sandy DuBois, for her editorial eye and nutritional expertise.

Tony Cook, the editor of the Binghamton University Alumni Journal, and Jackie Durbin, the editor of the Towson State University Alumni Newsletter, were kind enough to publish my call for transition stories to their graduates. I appreciate their generosity and cooperation.

Thanks to Niko Pfund and Despina Papazoglou Gimbel at New York University Press for always being on top of things and moving this project so quickly through the process.

My friend Kathleen Barber is a constant source of support, encouragement, and inspiration in all my writing efforts, and my mother, Alice Weinberg, has been a one-woman public relations office on my behalf.

Finally, a special thanks to my nieces and nephew—Allison, my musical consultant; Adam, and his Elvis energy; Megan, with her great sense of humor; Sarah, who is taking her first steps; and Dana, the first of the cousins to make the big step into college.

Introduction

Tomorrow is the big day—your college graduation. Are you ready? Ready to move on? Ready to leave your friends and the campus where you've worked and perhaps lived for the last few years? Some students are so anxious to get on with their lives that they start packing in February. Others put off even thinking about it. When the big day comes, they're often left with a lot of loose ends and not enough time to do all they still want to do. They sometimes leave (or are dragged out kicking and screaming) with frustration and regret. A

1

few students are so uneasy with the idea of graduating that they, like Zonker, search for their own ways to break the kiln, even flunking a course they need to graduate.

When I was a college senior, my friends and I used to talk, only half jokingly, about the world ending on June 3. That was how we felt. The world we knew and loved was ending with our graduation on June 3. For those of us with no definite plans, it felt as if we were walking off the end of the earth. Even those with grad school or job plans felt they were taking a big step away from what was comfortable and supportive.

This book is designed to help college students anticipate the changes ahead and better prepare for them. The transition from college to what happens next doesn't take place overnight. The process actually begins the day you enter college and continues until well after you graduate and begin to think of your new environment as home—your world—a place where you belong as you once belonged on your campus.

You each will deal with the transition at your own pace. I hope that this book gives you a roadmap for doing so. Whether you're terrified of the changes that lie ahead, want to avoid thinking about them, have a lot of mixed feelings, or are eagerly anticipating them, there are steps you can take to make a successful transition.

Each chapter deals with an aspect of the transition from college to what lies ahead. I'll suggest things you can begin to do *before* your senior year to put yourself on a path to a manageable transition. I'll also talk about ways to make the best use of your senior year. A number of personal thinking exercises are included at various points. Use these to clarify your past experiences and prepare for future challenges. Finally, the information provided will assist you in arriving safely on the other side of the transition and establishing a life for yourself there. The setting and the people around you will be changing. You may do some changing too. Be true to yourself in the process. Those changes should be by your choice and should move you in directions you want to go.

> Rose: You can't be nobody but who you are, Cory. That shadow wasn't nothing but you growing into yourself. You either got to grow into it or cut it down to fit you. But that's all you got to make life with.   —August Wilson, *Fences*[1]

A Final Thought

Those who have most recently gone through a transition have valuable thoughts and experiences to share. You will find the words and insights of recent graduates incorporated throughout this book.

Your generation of college graduates can play a similar role in future editions. I'd like to hear from you.

- Are there any topics that you feel should be discussed more fully?
- Are there additional issues that should be included?
- Do you have suggestions about books, videos, or other resources to add to the list at the end of the book?
- Are there any personal quotations or stories that you'd like to share with college students who will

follow you? (If you send any personal quotations or stories, please indicate whether you are willing to have us print them, in whole or in part, in future editions of *The Transition Guide for College Juniors and Seniors.*)

Please send suggestions and comments to Carol Weinberg, c/o New York University Press, 70 Washington Square South, New York, NY 10012-1091. You can also e-mail the author directly through the Internet—cweinber@goucher.edu.

Hello, I Must Be Going: The Transition Process

When I ask recent graduates what they remember about the time when they were approaching graduation, the responses range from one extreme — "I was terrified," "I was in denial. I blanked it out. I didn't pack until the day I had to be out" — to the other — "I couldn't wait to leave and get on with the real world." One graduate recognized that "the party was over," and still another describes the conflicting feelings graduation evoked.

> I was nervous about leaving because it was comfortable. I lived in the dorms for four years. Ate dorm food. Somebody was always doing things for me that way. So I remember thinking what it would be like to have my own place. I think I was ready for it.
>
> —C.T.

A major transition such as graduation from college isn't a single event like the commencement ceremony itself. It's a process that can take as long as six months to a year to two years to fully move through.[1] Lots of changes occur all at once. You'll shift from the role of college student to the role of worker or grad student or unemployed person (at least temporarily!). Your relationships will change—the people you're used to spending time with often scatter all over the country and beyond, your boyfriend or girlfriend may go off in another direction, you'll move farther away from your family or perhaps go back home after several years on your own. Your routines will change if, for example, you begin a job that requires you to commute a distance to be at work every morning by eight o'clock. The luxury of rolling out of bed at nine thirty to get to a ten o'clock class will be but a fond memory.

Assumptions about yourself and the world can also be disrupted by graduation. Perhaps your view of yourself as a top student will be challenged by being among so many other top students in graduate or professional school. Or maybe your assumptions about how you'll fare in the workforce will prove unfounded.

> The most surprising thing to me centered around the intimidation anxiety of the working world. Soon after employment I realized that, although I was younger than most of my coworkers, I felt competent and able to provide meaningful contributions. This was not what I had originally expected.   —P.J.

Graduation brings about a number of changes simultaneously. All these changes contribute to a "double whammy," a transition that's part of a string of transitions.[2] College graduation certainly qualifies for many as a multiple whammy! The transition process has been described as a time of suspended animation between your past and your future as you confront the gap that separates the two. Although you need to let go of, or separate from, the past, you can also use much of what you've learned there to help you deal with what lies ahead.[3]

I like to think of the transition process as a trapeze act during the time when you've let go of one swinging bar and you're hoping to catch the next. It helps if you've practiced hard and learned how to time your release, keep your eyes in the right place, position your body correctly, and remain calm and confident. And it also helps to have a net!

Don't wait until you're already flying through the air on your way from one trapeze bar to the next to learn the skills you need. Think about the transition early to plan for the change and take more control over it.

Starting Early

Most life experiences move from beginning to middle to end. Often beginnings are difficult, as you have to adapt to new situations and expectations. Middles are the most fun because you basically know the ropes yet can still be surprised and challenged. By the time you reach the end of an experience you may be bored, frustrated, or otherwise ready to go. Or you could be sad about an ending that you're not ready for.

Transitions resequence the order of events so that you have to deal with an ending and a beginning before getting to that more comfortable middle ground. Endings, such as graduation, can become so consuming that you don't take the time to get ready for the new beginning that will immediately follow. Take a look at your own style for approaching beginnings to help you prepare. This will give you valuable insight. Keep a journal during your first few months of any kind of major change, for example, moving to a new town or traveling abroad. Write about your experiences and how you feel. Describe the hurdles you overcome and how you meet people, learn the ropes, and grow to feel at home. Where do you find support, and how do you make use of it?

Reread these journal notes to identify patterns you have for dealing with beginnings. If you know these patterns, you can cut through some of the trial and error the next time. At the least, it can help you remember how you felt disoriented before and got through it. Though this information is best accumulated as you are experiencing the change, it can also be helpful to look back on past transitions in a structured way.

Exercise: The Transition In

Explore your transition into college as one source of information about your style for dealing with beginnings. Imagine a videotape in your head, and rewind it to the very first day you began college. As you think about each question below, jot down your responses. You could also talk into a tape recorder or use your thoughts as a basis for discussion with a friend.

What did you look like when you first arrived? What were your first thoughts, feelings, and reactions upon arriving? What were the first things you did and the first places you went, and why? How much was the college environment like or unlike the one you were coming from, and how did that seem to affect you?

_____

_____

_____

_____

_____

_____

_____

_____

_____

_____

_____

_____

_____

_____

_____

_____

_____

_____

_____

_____

_____

_____

_____

_____

_____

_____

_____

Who were your first friends, and how were they similar to, or different from, you? What was your basic lifestyle like that first year—laid back, into social activities and parties, focused on academics, spending a lot of time elsewhere, or a mixture? How did you spend your free time, and what did you do for fun?

_____

_____

_____

_____

_____

_____

_____

_____

_____

_____

_____

_____

_____

How were your relationships with your family and friends from high school affected? During your first year, which people, objects, events, and incidents made you feel more alone or alienated? During your first year, which people, objects, events, and incidents made you feel more comfortable? Who are your friends *now,* and how does your present circle of friends compare with your first friends on campus?

_____

_____

_____

_____

_____
_____
_____
_____
_____
_____
_____
_____
_____

What do your responses to these questions tell you about how you deal with beginnings? What would it help you to remember the next time you anticipate a transition?

_____
_____
_____
_____
_____
_____
_____
_____
_____
_____
_____
_____
_____

Preparing for the Transition throughout College

Reach beyond your college environment as often as you can. Take advantage of opportunities to learn about the experiences of recent college graduates. Friends and acquaintances who have graduated often come back to visit the campus. Find out what they're discovering out there and perhaps what they wish they had done differently while they were still at college. Take advantage of this information.

Perhaps your college offers the opportunity to study abroad. Participation in such a program can help you to learn how to take charge of your own life.

> My year abroad in Amsterdam was great preparation. No one takes you by the hand. It's like the ancient Greeks who left their babies out in the wilderness and if they crawled back to the civilization, they survived. If they didn't, they didn't.   —C.D.

In addition to a year or a semester studying abroad, some schools offer off-campus internships, trips during semester breaks, or the chance to spend a semester or a year as an exchange student at another college or university. Membership on a team or in an organization also provides opportunities to travel to other places for tournaments and conferences. Take advantage of these.

Use your early years in college to explore as many experiences as you can. You never know when something will take you in a new direction or give you experience that will make a future transition smoother. One graduate describes the impact an early internship had on her. This woman's freshman year had been a difficult one. She was very far from home and not totally happy at school. Her political science professor noticed her discomfort. He also saw that she really liked political science and was interested in government. This teacher was concerned that the student would go home for

January break and perhaps never come back, so he arranged an internship for her in Washington, D.C. That was a turning point. The student saw she was working for a goal—that everything was going to make sense. She worked every summer after that in Washington, and those connections helped her when she graduated. The experience also made Washington a less scary place for her to move to when she went looking for her first job after graduation.

Senior Year

> At the beginning of my senior year it didn't hit me that I'd be leaving. By March I was absolutely terrified. I was leaving everything that was safe. I knew once I graduated that nothing was gonna be the same again. And it wasn't. It was really terrifying not to know where I was gonna be living, what I was gonna be doing, and if you were in a relationship where that person was gonna be, whether it was gonna end, or just what was gonna happen.   —V.A.

It's often not until the senior year that the impending change begins to feel real (for example, that was the last time I'll ever register for classes here, that was my last room draw). Think about the transition *before* you have to actually make it. This can help you try on the change ahead and better prepare for it. One exercise I developed to help seniors do this uses the analogy of a bridge.[4]

Exercise: The Bridge

Close your eyes and imagine yourself planted firmly here at college, on this side of a bridge. From the safety of this side, I want to take you on a trip across that bridge—a trip that will let you visualize the transition ahead. This time you're just visiting—trying to learn what to expect so that when you go for real you can feel better prepared. Use my questions as a guide and the spaces provided periodically to jot down your thoughts and images.

How do you feel on this side of the bridge? How would you describe yourself? What roles and relationships define who you are in this environment? What is your physical setting like (rural, urban, isolated, modern)? Who makes up your support system (family, specific friends, girlfriend or boyfriend, teachers, counselors, teammates, or members of religious, cultural, or political groups)?

Now look ahead and visualize a bridge in front of you. This is the bridge you'll be taking after you graduate. It's your own personal bridge. Can you see where it leads, or is the other side hidden by a fog? Is it a long bridge that seems to go a great distance, or is it a relatively quick trip from here to there? What does the bridge look like? Is it wide, with lots of lanes, or narrow? As you look at your bridge, does it look sleek and firm and steady? Does it inspire confidence? Or is it a more shaky bridge with some old planks that make you wonder if you'll make it safely across? Do you see much other traffic? Does it seem that you're traveling in the same direction as others, or do you feel as if you're really taking an uncharted course?

_____

_____

_____

_____

_____

_____

_____

_____

_____

_____

_____

_____

_____

_____

Get ready to begin to cross your bridge. How will you be traveling? On foot? In a vehicle? If you're on foot—walking or jogging or running—how does that feel? If you're in a vehicle, describe the vehicle. Are you driving, or is someone else behind the wheel? Why did you choose the mode of travel you did?

Is anyone else with you on this trip—actually or in spirit? What is the view like as you travel across your bridge? Can you see anything in particular ahead of you or behind you? How about over the sides? What kind of pace are you traveling at? How do you feel as you make the trip? Are you heading toward something permanent or something temporary? How much in control of the trip do you feel? If you'd like to feel more control, what would it take to help you feel that?

_____

_____

_____

_____

_____

_____

Visualize yourself arriving at the other end of your bridge. What do you feel as you get there? What roles and relationships do you expect to have there? How are these similar to, or different from, those you had at college? What is the physical setting like? How is this setting similar to or different from the one you left? Look around. Is anyone you know already there? Where do you see your potential support system coming from? When you think about your own style for dealing with beginnings, what are the first things you want to do in this new place? How will you begin to build the connections you need?

_____

_____

_____

_____

_____

_____

_____

_____

_____

_____

_____

_____

running back and forth across my bridge several times a day. And it was a long bridge! As soon as I set aside specific days to focus on one side or the other, I was much more productive at both ends. Plan on specific times to concentrate on future plans and other times to tie up loose ends at college.

Exercise: If Tomorrow Were Graduation Day

This is it. The night before your graduation. Imagine that after the ceremony tomorrow you'll be whisked off, never to return. Are there any

1. places on campus or in the area you've always wanted to go but haven't (e.g., an art museum, a mountain)? _____
   _____
   _____

2. places that have been especially meaningful or important to you that you want to visit one last time (e.g., where you met your boyfriend or girlfriend, or a homeless shelter where you volunteered during your junior year)? ____
   _____
   _____

3. things you've wanted to do but haven't done yet (e.g., bicycle to the state park, talk with a particular professor about her or his research)? _____
   _____
   _____

4. things you've enjoyed doing and want to do one last time (e.g., stay up all night with friends and watch the sun rise, jog with a friend)? _____
   _____
   _____

Well, since it's not really the night before your graduation, you still have time to act on these wishes. Look back over your responses and plan to actually do some of these things or go some of these places before you leave.

There's a certain amount of loss involved in leaving a place that's important to you. Acknowledge what you value about your college and college experience. Celebrate what you'll miss, and bid a joyous farewell to what you won't. This may help you let go, say good-bye, and take positive memories with you.

1. If you could fill a backpack with things to take with you (e.g., snack bar milk shakes, sophomore year intramural softball team, your psych professor's annoying but challenging questions), what would you take, and why? _____

    _____

    _____

    _____

2. What or who will it be hardest for you to let go of, say good-bye to, and leave behind? _____

    _____

    _____

    _____

3. What or who will you be thrilled to never see or hear again? _____

    _____

    _____

    _____

4. What do you hope stays the same, and what do you hope will change about your college in the future? _____

_____

_____

_____

5. What did you contribute (to individuals or to the institution) during your time here? _____

    _____

    _____

    _____

Consider some kind of ceremony to acknowledge these things. For example, one year when I worked in the residence halls, two seniors and I put together a time capsule using a Tupperware bread box to hold mementos of our valued experiences. One student was the editor of the college paper, and she included ·several issues. The other had directed a play on campus, and she contributed the program. We stood outside in the drizzle in the middle of the night and buried the Tupperware time capsule outside the residence hall where I lived. We made little speeches about what we'd learned and how we'd grown, and we told some funny stories and laughed a lot. Then we took a walk around the campus (a victory lap?!). We felt we'd left our mark by celebrating our accomplishments in a concrete way.

Making the Transition

Once you get to the other side of your bridge, look at how your roles, relationships, routines, and assumptions about yourself and the world are changing, and identify the resources you have for coping with these changes.[6]

> The first month or so I think I was in shock. I moved to a foreign country and was living with my boyfriend for the first time, and everything was so new and bizarre I really didn't have much time to absorb it. It was both hugely liberating and overwhelming. I felt much freer than I had in college, and alternately frightened and excited about not having a clear sense of direction. I had really enjoyed college, but I had been a very serious academic and had not really enjoyed the party scene. My first few jobs were in restaurants, and I found myself living a rather bohemian lifestyle. I don't know if I would have been so bold on my own without knowing that my boyfriend and I were looking out for each other. I don't think I could live that way again, but I am very glad to have experienced it. I think I enjoyed it fully because I knew it was temporary.   —M.M.

One graduate describes her first reaction to life after college as "feeling like a freshman again." In a sense you are a freshman again. What's different, however, is the knowledge and skill you bring with you based on your college experience. Don't minimize the value of what you've already learned.

Your own personal evaluation of a transition determines how you handle it. If you see the change as one for the better, then you're more likely to cope with it effectively.[7] Look at the change in your role in terms of resulting gains and losses. If you perceive the gains as greater than the losses, then the transition will be more easily managed.

> I was looking forward to having a job and an apartment and to not packing up and moving or storing my stuff every year. I was looking forward to the independence and stability. For months the only time I was off campus was when I played in a lacrosse game. I was looking forward to having space to live in. I had

gone from growing up in a large farm house to sharing a dorm room with another person. I was eager to get into an apartment. I didn't have to do homework and I had more control over everything I did.   —S.S.

Generally, the more similarity there is between your new and old roles and environments, the easier the transition should be.[8] For example, if you're gladly going directly on to be a graduate student, that should be an easier transition than going to a nonstudent role such as office worker or parent. One way to ease the latter kind of transition is to assume a variety of roles in different environments during college—perhaps hold a part-time job in an office during school or in the summer, or do some babysitting or volunteer work with children.

Life at college often creates routines (dinner between 5:00 p.m. and 7:00 p.m., shooting pool on Saturday afternoons, wandering around at 2:00 a.m. to hang out with people, syllabi, and due dates for school work). If having a comfortable routine gives you a sense of security, the change in those routines can create some stress.

Your new situation may replace college structures with new ones, or you may need to create some routines for yourself. One Penn State graduate describes her early days after relocating to Boston. She structured a routine for herself that focused around getting to know her new city and exploring the job market there. There may also be some old routines, such as doing the Sunday paper crossword puzzle or working out three times a week, that you can incorporate into your new life. On the other hand, some students are also thrilled to feel less imposed structure and more control over their own time.

The ability to cope with a transition is also affected by your own personal resources and the support of others. Take time to identify and appreciate your strengths *before* you begin the transition. This may help you maintain perspective if the trip across the bridge gets rough. Consider characteristics and strengths such as your

flexibility
sense of humor
resilience
optimistic approach to life
good feelings about yourself
fighting spirit
ability to identify personal strengths
ability to catch negative self-descriptions and put them
   in perspective
skill at analyzing situations, generating options, and
   planning and implementing changes[9]

Develop these kinds of personal resources. They'll be beneficial throughout many life transitions. One way to explore personal strengths and resources is to use assessment tools such as the Myers-Briggs Personality Inventory. This instrument helps you explore your style of dealing with the world and making decisions and is a great way to clarify and help you appreciate your strengths.[10] Many college counseling centers and career development offices offer the Myers-Briggs and an interpretation of the results. (The book *Please Understand Me,* by David Keirsey and Marilyn Bates, also adapts the Myers-Briggs concepts.)

Because a transition can throw you off balance, identify some anchors for yourself to serve as a point of reference. For example, I was part of several groups that ended the year by giving one another written "gifts" of appreciation. We each walked away with a paper bag full of notes telling us what other people really liked about us. I have often taken out those bags and read through my strengths in others' eyes when I was starting to lose sight of them myself.

One graduate describes the difference between finding support at college and finding it in the real world. "In college," he says, "you have support groups flung at you. In real life you have to fling yourself at them." Support from others is vital for a successful transition. This means having people in your life who care about you, who can support your choices and decisions, and who will help you in a crisis.[11] Support comes from a variety of sources—family, friends, partners, institutions, and organizations (for example, professional organizations or twelve-step programs). Some sources of support will always be there for you, regardless of where you go and what you're doing. Others may fade as your situation changes. They may be replaced by new supports within your new environment. (Chapter 2 discusses friends and relationships in more detail.)

Exercise: Your Support System

A support system will include your closest friends and relationships but will also go beyond that. Different people can provide you with different kinds of support. Some provide a variety of things, and others may offer only one thing, but that could be something you don't receive from anyone else. You may also find some gaps in your current support system.[12] For each of the statements listed below, write the name or names of those who currently provide that type of support to you.

1. I feel close to them. _____
    _____

2. I can discuss personal concerns with them. _____
    _____

3. I can count on them in a crisis. _____
    _____

4. They make me feel good about myself. _____
    _____

5. They challenge my thinking. _____
    _____

6. They will be honest with me. _____
    _____

7. I can share good news with them. _____
    _____

8. They introduce me to new ideas and perspectives. _____
    _____

Think back to the exercise earlier in this chapter in which you crossed your transitional bridge. Did you see any of these people crossing along with you? Consider the kind of support they provide. How will you maintain your connections to them in the future? As you make your transition, how will you find new supports to supplement those that become less accessible to you?

Some Final Words

As you approach your transition out of college, remember that this is only a first step. You could end up staying for the rest of your life where this transition takes you, or you may cross other bridges later on.

I asked a number of people who have been through their own transitions what they would say to a college senior approaching graduation if they could tell them one thing. Here's what some of them said.

It takes at least a couple of years before things begin to shake out. Keep on plugging.   —H.M.

I gained a lot of self-confidence from the transition process and learned that I can rely on myself and survive.   —F.J.

Don't be afraid to take risks. Those experiences change you forever. Do them while you can—when you don't have a lot of other responsibilities yet. Venture off on your own for a while.

—M.L.

It's not gonna be like school, so be ready to accept what comes and make the best out of it. Look at it as an adventure where you have to discover everything as you go. And enjoy the discovery of it.

—B.S.

Do what you feel, what's in your heart. Be wary of advice, even this advice.   —D.J.

That's What Friends Are For: Friends and Relationships

I had the sense that I would never have the opportunity to have as many good friends as I did all within walking distance or campus phone distance again. I also knew the strong relationships would be maintained and that happened.   —M.J.

One of my most vivid memories of my senior year was how a group of people who had been coworkers (we were all R.A.'s) came together as close friends during our last semester. As one of them described that time: "We sang and danced and ate and drank. We talked and walked into gray 5 a.m. dawns past long-ago and yet to come." [1] At times it felt as if we were trying to cram in as much good time together as we possibly could before we had to leave. The closer graduation got, the more intense about it we became. This was where my "the world ends June 3" feeling came from. Part of what I didn't want to leave was college life; part was the feeling of having these good people around me. This sentiment is echoed in the movie *The Big Chill,* when the Glenn Close character tells her old college friends, "I feel like I was at my best with you people."

Starting Early

College is surely a time when a world of potential friends encircles you. Take advantage of the opportunities the college experience offers to get to know a variety of people. Life in a residence hall, in a fraternity or sorority house, or in a house with other students creates a ready-made start. It takes effort from both sides to work at a friendship, and when you see someone every day (in the residence hall, in class, at team practice), that helps speed things along. There's also a domino effect that can expand your social circle of potential friends.

- Your chem lab partner lives in a different area of campus and invites you to a party there.
- Your roommate has a boyfriend or a girlfriend at another college and asks if you want to study over there and meet some folks for coffee.
- Your R.A. works on the school yearbook and asks for volunteers to stay up all night helping the staff meet a deadline.

You may already have experienced the effects of transition on friendship as a result of your move from high school to college. Perhaps some of your high school friends have remained your friends throughout college. You may have drifted away from others as you got involved in college life and developed new relationships there. Take time to think about what's important to you in a friendship. This can help you make decisions about where to put your energy as you move on, because it does take effort to build and maintain a relationship.

> My best friend and I both make a concerted effort to make regular visits. I see her once a year and we talk every four to six weeks—two-hour-long conversations. In those conversations we bring each other up to date from day-to-day to the most far-reaching problems.   —C.C.

Exercise: Friendship Patterns

Look at the people who have been your good friends and how those friendships have developed. This can help you be alert to potential new friends in your world after college. List on the numbered lines below the names of four to six friends who have been really important to you *at some point in your life.* Then, under each friend's name, respond to the questions listed below.

a. How long have you have known this person?
b. Where and how did you first meet her or him?
c. When was the last time you had contact with him or her, and what did you do or talk about?
d. What do you value the most about this person?
e. What do you get from this friendship?
f. What do you give to this friendship?

For example:

1. Gabriella
   a. Two years.
   b. Met in a social psychology class when we worked on a group project together.

c. Saw her last week and we went out for pizza and talked about grad school applications and just hung out together.

d. She makes me think about things in new ways.

e. I get intellectually challenged by her and she also supports me as I'm trying to figure out my career direction.

f. I don't know. I guess I do the same for her.

2. Lloyd

a. Since third grade—about twelve years.

b. We lived next door to one another and used to play all the time when we were kids.

c. I can't remember when the last time was we talked—maybe about a year or so ago. We talked about what we were both doing now but mostly about old times. He also told me about some personal stuff he was struggling with.

d. He's always there for me if I need him. I don't have to explain everything or try to be anything I'm not.

e. I get a sense of security from him, a link to my childhood, and a lot of laughs.

f. I give him someone he can count on and trust. I also push him to go after the things he wants.

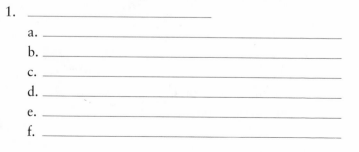

1. _____

    a. _____

    b. _____

    c. _____

    d. _____

    e. _____

    f. _____

2. _____

    a. _____

    b. _____

    c. _____

    d. _____

    e. _____

    f. _____

3. _____

    a. _____

    b. _____

    c. _____

    d. _____

    e. _____

    f. _____

4. _____

    a. _____

    b. _____

    c. _____

    d. _____

    e. _____

    f. _____

5. _____

    a. _____

    b. _____

    c. _____

    d. _____

    e. _____

    f. _____

6. _____

    a. _____

    b. _____

c. _____

d. _____

e. _____

f. _____

You can expand this exercise to look at the scope of your friendship patterns by including additional information such as each friend's gender, religion, ethnic background, socio-economic class, sexual orientation, and age.

Review your list to get a sense of the patterns of your important friendships. Are there ways or places you usually meet the people who have become your friends? Do you both give and get important things from the relationships? Do you know what you give others? If you're not sure, ask them. Do you stay in touch with good friends? Is there anyone you want to contact after doing this exercise?

Do your friendships cross over demographic lines, or is the circle of your friends fairly limited? Take advantage of opportunities to meet both people who share common interests with you and those who are different in some ways. You may have some friends with whom you do particular things (for example, your jogging friend or the friend you go to concerts with), and others who are there for you at a deep personal level. You don't need to approach every friendship thinking about making that person your best friend forever. Those relationships that grow will be the special ones.

There are two friends I still have from college. One was my old roommate, and he and I shared a lot of experiences together. The other is just a genuinely good person who always supported me and never really expected anything from me. Just allowed me to be who I was. I think that's just the most beautiful kind of person you can run into. We met in our first acting class together first semester, then sort of went through the college experience together. We remain constant with each other.   —C.D.

Senior Year

The process of dealing with endings and good-byes is another one for which we each have a style. Some folks, like the Motown song says, "never can say good-bye." Others prefer to find some closure. Good-byes and tying up loose ends with people you really care about can be difficult. Don't let the difficulty keep you from doing it.

Move beyond the circle of your closest friends and also seek out individuals who have been important to you in some way and tell them what they've given you. This could include acquaintances, teachers, staff members, coaches, the janitors in your residence hall, security officers, and the cook in the dining hall.

Think also about any individual you've left something unsaid with (maybe a former roommate or an old girlfriend or boyfriend) and consider whether you want to talk to her or him before you leave to resolve any unfinished business. This could mean, for example, apologizing for something, telling someone that they've hurt you along the way, or working through an old conflict so you don't leave with bad feelings about one another. This could also mean telling someone that they've taught you something important or made a positive difference in your life.

Many colleges give seniors opportunities to celebrate their

last time together. Some have a series of activities and events culminating in graduation. This senior week offers a time to enjoy the campus and the company of your classmates without the pressures of academic work. Events, trips, and parties provide the chance to celebrate the four years, tie up loose ends, and strengthen connections.

When I anticipate having to say good-bye to a good friend, I try to develop enough momentum in the relationship to keep it running until we can get back together. It's kind of like charging the battery in your car so it will run on its own. Hopefully, that charge will keep it going until we can talk to one another or see one another again and recharge our batteries.

Use your senior year to charge up those batteries well. Spend time with the people most important to you. Talk about your relationship and how you can keep in touch if you're going in different directions after graduation. Plan ahead of time for a first visit or phone call after you part.

> I still feel very close to the few friends I stay in touch with. I haven't seen them in well over a year, and we probably don't write or call as much as we should, but somehow the bond remains. We all have commented on how it's strange that even though we are not always up to date on our current lives, we feel closer to each other than we do to some friends we see regularly. I think it's because we established a true emotional intimacy while at school, and the love and affection is strong enough to withstand distance and time.   —M.M.

Making the Transition

Moving On

The challenge as you make the transition out of college is to maintain the close friends who are important to you, yet not become so dependent on old friends that you close yourself off to new possibilities. This same challenge has been there during other life transitions, but it may be more difficult as you move out of the student role. Going from college to real life is different from moving from high school to college.

Develop your skills at meeting people. There are few settings with as many ready-made opportunities as you had in college. It takes a greater effort to meet new people outside the school setting. One graduate describes how she moved to a new city and lived with several old friends there. They went out as a group regularly to the same one or two places. By going together it was easier to get comfortable in a strange, new city. Once this graduate was familiar with the new places, however, she made it a point to go back at times on her own. This allowed her to be more open to meeting new people as an individual rather than always being part of a group.

The balance of old and new is important. One recent graduate describes moving back to his hometown after graduation. He not only had his college friends, but also some of his original high school friends and his family, *plus* the new friends he was meeting in law school and through his community activities.

Staying Nearby

Some graduates ease the transition by spending the summer with friends before everyone heads off in different directions. The roles may be changed, but the routines will stay the same for a while longer. Other students decide to assume their new roles (perhaps as a grad student or a worker) in the same geographic area—in a town or a city that's familiar to them. A few may even work on campus for the summer or for a year or two. Many schools, for example, use a recent graduate or two in their admissions office.

If you stay near your college area, recognize that you're no longer a student. That may be harder to do if you're living with the same people and following similar routines to those you followed as an undergraduate. Create some new routines and seek out new experiences and acquaintances.

In the movie *St. Elmo's Fire,* for example, a group of seven close friends who just graduated from Georgetown University together remain inseparable during the year after they graduate. They all continue to live in Washington, D.C., and though all are working, or trying to work, they still live with and depend on each other. They even congregate regularly at their old table at St. Elmo's Pub. At the end of the movie, one character finally decides to leave for New York. The rest see him off at the bus station, and this first break allows others to begin to take steps forward. One woman, for example, tells the two men who have been competing for her love that she needs time for herself away from both of them even though they'll remain friends. The six characters left agree, at the end of the movie, to meet for brunch the next Sunday, but not at St. Elmo's. "Let's go to another place that's less noisy and doesn't have as many kids," one of them suggests, and all agree. They've taken an important step.

Letting Go and Learning What Lasts

After graduation there's a tendency for friends to drift apart if they get very involved in their new lives. It's most difficult if one friend makes this shift while the other doesn't. One graduate talks about initially staying close to friends still in the area but then finding that, as they developed different goals and worldviews, they tended to drift apart. People find and establish their own lives, and that can mean letting go of some of the past. But there's always the possibility of reconnecting again. For example, as hard as I find it to leave very close friends, it's even more exhilarating when I see someone after a year or two and discover that we've been moving in parallel rather than divergent directions. Not only do we have our original strong bonds, but we now have lots to share with one another that we can both understand and appreciate.

I've often asked graduates what made the difference in those relationships that have lasted the longest for them after graduation. Shared activities and common experiences in college helped to build those bonds. So did going through similar problems. Another graduate discovered that she actually got closer to some folks who had been just acquaintances in college when they began to share the graduate school experience.

The people I stayed close to share the same love and respect for our college. We also went through similar things at work, even though we were working at different places. I also remained

closest to those who followed similar paths—working, getting
married. And it helps when friends like their friends' husbands.

—C.C.

Keeping in Touch

Some friends keep in touch by writing, but sometimes it's
hard to find the time to do that. Make use of dead time
(waiting for your clothes in the laundromat or commuting by
train) to get some correspondence done. Telephone calls are
also a good way of staying in touch but not always affordable, especially if you're on a tight budget. You may also
wind up talking more to an answering machine than to the
friend you're trying to reach. If both you and your friend are
working at places that are on the Internet, or can access
it from home computers, e-mail provides additional casual
communication opportunities.

College reunions offer a chance to reconnect with old
friends if you all choose to attend. One graduate also found
that during the first couple of years after graduation several
people from her group of friends got married. Those wed-
dings served as minireunions. The friends would all pile into
one apartment or hotel room and catch up with one another's
lives.

Another graduate gets together every six months or so
with her college friends, and they plan one trip they take
together sometime during each year. These kinds of group
efforts can be hard to organize, however, if people have
divergent schedules, are widely separated geographically, and
are coming from economically different situations. You don't

necessarily have to keep in close touch to feel connected. I've found a few rare friendships that continue even though we're only able to recharge our batteries by mail once a year and in person as infrequently as once in ten years.

> There are some people you can go away from for years and you come back and you'll be the same way because there's that understanding between you.   —C.D.

Relationships

Doonesbury, copyright by G. B. Trudeau. Reprinted with permission of Universal Press Syndicate. All rights reserved.

If you're involved in a serious relationship with someone at college, graduation can create some anxiety. Individual choices are complicated enough, but they can be even more difficult if you're trying to coordinate two sets of plans. If you're both pursuing careers, decisions about moves are likely to recur throughout your life together. What if the two of you have offers in different places? Whose offer takes priority? What does that mean for the other partner? You may graduate together and go to different places, or one of you may graduate first.

> The hardest thing I had to deal with was leaving my fiancé, who was a junior when I graduated. Even though we were only an hour apart, there were other things that compounded the challenges of a long-distance relationship. My fiancé was pursuing a double major in biology and nursing, and he was also on a four-year scholarship in basketball. Playing basketball required him to be out of town, and when he wasn't out of town, he had to adjust his schedule to include practice time, home games, time to make up work that he had missed while he was on the road, time to study, and also time for me. To say the least, this was a very stressful period during our relationship; however, we conquered the challenges, and we made it through.   —B.T.

Some students in a serious relationship feel a push to formalize a commitment as graduation looms ahead. While that decision can feel more secure, it's not one to be made quickly. Other partners work at long-distance relationships, traveling to spend time with one another whenever possible. There are certainly some risks involved in being in different places and creating individual lives for yourselves. One or both of you may decide that the relationship isn't right for you any more, or that you need some freedom before making a long-term commitment. But two fully realized individuals choosing to be together is more productive in the long run than a premature engagement or marriage.

Even if you and your partner go to the same place after graduation, and perhaps live together, if your roles or routines change, this will likely have an impact on the relationship. One graduate describes feeling a lot of anxiety about how she and her boyfriend would fare after graduation. They were moving to the same city but into potentially different worlds. One of them was going to be a grad student, and the other would be working full time. If you're making the transition with a partner, discuss beforehand how you'll approach this new stage in your relationship. Be honest about your fears and concerns.

Can You Go Home Again?

If you feel ties to your campus or to people who are still there, you may be tempted to go back at some point, especially if you're not that far away. It can be risky, however, to go back before you've begun to develop a new life for yourself on the other side of your bridge. If the college side of your bridge feels much more attractive, maintaining your focus there can interfere with devoting the necessary energy to your new world. I always made it a point to wait about a year before I went back to visit any place I had loved and left. If you've begun to create some ties and roots on the other side of the bridge, then you can more safely go back for a visit, knowing that there's something to look forward to that draws you back where you now belong, on the other side.

Memories from a distance also minimize the negatives and exaggerate the positives. A visit back to your school is sometimes disappointing. You'll walk across a campus where you once felt totally at home and see very few people you recognize. You may feel replaced as others now fill the roles you once filled, such as diver on the swim team or president of your residence hall. I've seen graduates returning for their twenty-fifth reunions go looking to see "their" rooms. It can be a sobering experience to go back if you haven't already established some new roles for yourself.

> Holly: You know, for the past six years I have been afraid to see any of you. Mostly because I haven't made any specific choices. My parents used to call me three times a week at 7 a.m. to ask me, "Are you thin, are you married to a root-canal man, are *you* a root-canal man?" And I'd hang up and wonder how much longer I was going to be in "transition." I guess since college I've missed the comfort and acceptance I felt with all of you. And I thought you didn't need that anymore, so I didn't see you.
> —Wendy Wasserstein, *Uncommon Women and Others*[2]

If you return to campus while there are still a lot of students there who remember you, a visit back can be frantic. How do you see everyone you want to? How do you avoid being pulled into a variety of unwanted directions when there are specific people you want to see and things you want to do? One graduate describes staying with friends off campus and just calling the people he wanted to see.

The ideal is to go back to visit, if you do, with a sense of perspective—able to enjoy your time back, accept the changes there (even if they may hurt a bit), and feel satisfied with where you are now and the direction in which you're headed.

THREE

Do You Know the Way to San Jose? Relocating

I've learned, through trial, error, and a bit of embarrassment, that to get a New York City malted in New Hampshire I had to order a frappé, and that ordering a hoagie with *everything* on it in Philadelphia included the hottest hot peppers I'd ever tasted. My biggest readjustment came when I moved from the East to graduate school in the Midwest. People commented about my funny accent. My tendency to tease people wasn't funny to some of my new acquaintances. When someone asked me if I wanted a Vernors, I wasn't sure what I was saying OK to. It turned out to be a kind of ginger ale. The cashier in a store asked me if I wanted a sack for my purchase. "No, a bag is fine," I told her. She looked at me as if I was talking a different language. I was.

Starting Early

Sometimes you'll have control over where you go after college. You'll choose to remain in the same general area or to relocate to a new place or perhaps to go back home. Other times you'll have less choice. Perhaps you'll go to the graduate school that gives you the best financial aid package or relocate where your employer assigns you or accompany your partner to her or his new location. If you have some choice about where you relocate, there are a variety of issues to consider.

Exercise: The Best of All Possible Worlds

Imagine that you're the head of the chamber of commerce in your ideal city or town—the place where you'd most like to live after you graduate. Describe that environment so that someone who has never been there can get a good idea of what the place is like.

1. Where in the United States or in the world is it? _____
_____

2. How large (area and population) is it? _____
_____

3. Is your ideal location city, suburban, rural, in the mountains, near the ocean, or what? _____
_____

4. What is the climate like there? In the summer? In the winter? _____
_____

5. How accessible is this place via car, train, bus, plane (especially to family and friends with whom you want to maintain contact)? _____
_____

6. What kind of public transportation is there? _____
_____

7. What cultural facilities are available (theaters, museums, concerts)? _____

_____

8. What sports and recreation facilities are available? _____

_____

9. Which professional sports teams, if any, are in this area?

_____

10. What opportunities for additional education are available? _____

_____

11. What is the population like (average age, singles or families, ethnic diversity, socioeconomic levels)? _____

_____

12. How do people who live here treat one another? _____

_____

13. What does it cost to live here? _____

_____

Once you've come up with your ideal responses, place each of them into one of the following three categories.

1. Most important to you

_____

_____

_____

_____

2. Important, but not crucial

_____

_____

_____

_____

3. Not very important

_____

_____

_____

_____

The description of your most important criteria should give you a picture of the type of location where you would most like to relocate. Several books available in the library can tell you about various places and let you evaluate different locations based on your preferred criteria. *The Places Rated Almanac,* for example, ranks and compares all 343 officially designated metropolitan areas in North America (the United States and Canada) on the basis of ten factors that influence the quality of living: cost of living, job outlook, housing, transportation, education, health care, crime, the arts, recreation, and climate. The *Inter-City Cost of Living Index,* published by the United States Chambers of Commerce, gives statistics for almost 300 cities.

If you're considering job offers in different locations, remember that the same salary may buy more in some places than others. Housing costs, taxes, heating and cooling expenses, transportation, and so forth, all vary from location to location. A smaller salary in some cities, therefore, could be as good as or better than a larger salary in a city where apartments are more expensive, commuting and parking costs are greater, and you need to constantly have your heat turned up.[1]

I was planning to go to a graduate school in the same area where I went to undergraduate school, but another two or three years in the same place seemed like a step backwards to me. Going back to the safety of everything I already knew could have been easy, but not challenging.   —G.J.

You may want to stay, after you graduate, in the vicinity of your college or return to the area where you grew up or somewhere you lived before. Familiarity can breed comfort. While it's nice to feel comfortable, there's such a thing as getting too comfortable and never trying something new. One graduate cites his decision to move away from his college town to work a distance away as the most productive decision he made. It was important, he said, for him to move away from the parties and the college environment in order to feel that he could throw himself fully into his postgraduate life.

If you've had limited experience with different locations, consider how to broaden your experience before you graduate and have to make a decision about where to go. Summers and vacation breaks during your college years provide opportunities for you to visit different parts of the country. Seek out summer jobs in new and different places. Look into trips your college offers during summer and semester breaks. If you meet friends at college who come from different areas of the country, perhaps you can go home with them on a vacation and they can join you for another. At the least, talk to classmates from different places. This will help you learn more about where they're from. Bear in mind, though, that even people who have lived someplace for a long time can have a limited view of their own home.

If you're on a college team (for example, athletic or debate), there will be opportunities to go to away games or contests.

Use these trips to gather information. Regional or national conferences for college students involved in particular organizations or activities (sororities or fraternities, community service, student government, cultural groups) provide similar opportunities. If you visit other campuses, include at least a quick look at the neighboring community. Anytime you find yourself in an airport between connections with time to kill, pick up a local newspaper and get a feel for what's going on there.

As you gather all this information, you may decide that there are some places you definitely wouldn't want to move to, others that have possibilities for you, and some that you really like. Store away this information and consider it later in your college career as you begin to look more seriously at your plans for after graduation.

Senior Year

By your senior year, you're probably narrowing down your relocation possibilities. If finding a job is your top priority (either an open-ended search or within some geographical limits), then you'll be focusing on the job and dealing with relocation issues after you get that job. Or you may be considering location first, planning to look for a job in that location after you've moved. Perhaps you've decided to buy some time or save some money by staying in the area of your college for the summer or returning to your parents' house. If you take advantage of either of the last two options, set some goals and timelines for them. For example, your goal for the summer could be to do a concentrated job hunt or to choose an area to move to by August 15. A sublet that ends by August 31 or an understanding with your parents that you're home until the end of August will help to keep you on deadline. You can always decide to extend the date, depending on circumstances, but open-ended temporary plans can sometimes turn into dead-end permanent situations unless you take an active approach.

Check It Out

If you have access to the Internet at your college, you can search for information about specific cities through networks such as Netscape. There are also many travel guides in the library and in bookstores. These will tell you a lot about different areas of the country and parts of the world. If you or your parents belong to the American Automobile Association (AAA), you can order a tour book that gives information about specific states. Your college alumni office may also be willing to give you the names of alumni in the area where you're heading. They can provide additional information as you finalize your choices, and there may be a local chapter in your new location that would serve as a good contact once you arrive.

To find out how compatible the locations you're considering are to your own needs, seek information from some specialized outside sources. For example, if you want to know about the accessibility of an area and compliance with the Americans with Disabilities Act, contact the National Council on Independent Living (703-525-3406). Request a free copy of their "Independent Living Center Directory." Then call centers in the areas you're considering relocating to and ask them for information.

If you want information about civil rights protection for homosexuals, try the National Gay and Lesbian Task Force (202-332-6483). As of 1995, California, Connecticut, Hawaii, Massachusetts, Minnesota, New Jersey, Rhode Island, Vermont, and Wisconsin had legislation providing such protection.[2]

Data about bias incidents or hate crimes can be obtained from several sources. Klanwatch, a project of the Southern Poverty Law Center, publishes both a bimonthly newsletter and a yearly report that lists, by city and state, active hate groups and reported bias incidents (racist, homophobic, anti-Semitic, and so forth). If you contact them (400 Washington Avenue, Montgomery, AL 36104; 205-264-0286), they will send you a copy. The Anti-Defamation League of B'nai B'rith monitors anti-Semitic activity and also publishes an annual report (823 United Nations Plaza, New York, NY 10017; 212-490-2525).

For information about services and resources within your religious denomination, start with a clergyperson you trust — a chaplain at your college, someone from the off-campus community, or someone from back home. Tell them where you're thinking of moving, and ask if they know any clergy in that location you can contact. Check out several different congregations. Talk also with the lay people who serve as the governing body (for example, the vestry or the parish council). Conversations with staff in charge of various programs — educational, community service, music, young adult ministries—can tell you whether the congregation offers the types of activities and events that mesh with your priorities.

I've always found that secondary information cannot replace the experience of checking places out for yourself, if that's at all possible. If you travel to a potential job or grad school site for an interview, build in time to explore the area—maybe stay an extra day if you can. Walk or ride around and try it on for size. How would you feel living there? Sit in a coffee shop or a park and listen to the conversations. Wander through the library. Do some window shopping. Read the posters on the bulletin board in the supermarket. Visit a place of worship. Look for the kinds of places you like to hang out, and get a feel for what they're like in this location. What do you see that looks new and different and interesting? When you leave, do you find that you're glad to get out of there, or do you feel kind of interested and excited? You may be nervous even if you're excited; any change, even a good one, involves a certain amount of anxiety. I remember pacing up and down in the Hartford/Springfield airport after an interview for one particular job. I instinctively knew that this job was the right move for me to make after eight years at my then-current position. I knew that if they offered it to me I'd take it. I was excited, but I was also scared to death of the big change it would mean.

Once you know where you're relocating, focus your information-gathering process. Local chambers of commerce or offices of tourism will often provide relocation packets that contain information about apartments, real estate, local government, services and agencies, events, medical facilities, libraries, recreational facilities, educational institutions, the economy and businesses of the area, the population, transportation, and shopping. Keep in mind, however, that these materials are designed to show off the best features of an area. They may also be biased toward the companies that belong to the chamber of commerce. If you're moving somewhere to work for a company or a business, that organization may provide its own relocation materials. Request the information you want if none is offered.

As you narrow down your location choices, or once a job or graduate school acceptance settles that question, learn as much as you can about your new home. Let friends, professors, and family know where you're heading. Often people will know people who are already there. Take names and numbers. You don't *have* to call or meet these people, but it's nice to have those contacts in case you want or need them.

Before You Leave

As you prepare to leave college, there are some practical matters to take care of. Have your mail forwarded to your new address. The post office has official change-of-address booklets. They include a change-of-address order to be sent to your current postmaster and several notification cards you can send to people who should know of the change. If you make a temporary move or two first, you may become an expert at doing these! Should you leave your college address before you have a new permanent one, you may temporarily forward mail to yourself in care of your parents or a friend in your new location. If you have a job but no place to live yet, it may be acceptable to temporarily have mail sent to you in care of your employer. Obtain permission first, though.

You can also have your mail held for you at the post office in your new location for up to thirty days. To do this, find out the zip code of your new post office. On the change-of-address order, under new address, write "c/o General Delivery," the name of your new post office station branch, and the zip code. Your current post office can help you locate the correct information. If you use general delivery, you'll need to call for your mail once a week. Once you have moved and found a permanent address, fill out another change-of-address card.

You'll need to change your address on any magazine subscriptions you have. It often takes four to six weeks for an address change to be processed through the publishers' computers.[3] As soon as you have a forwarding address, use an address label from your current subscription to tape onto the old address space on the notification cards. Many magazines have a form inside each issue for you to use with a current label for this purpose.

Credit card, bank, and other statements have special boxes to check to indicate a change in address. If you use a post office notification card instead, be sure to include your account number. Do you belong to any book, music, or video clubs that automatically send the monthly selection unless you notify them otherwise? If so, you need to cancel those memberships, suspend them temporarily, or notify them by letter of the effective date of your upcoming move. Keep a copy of the letter and send it "return receipt requested." This could avoid the hassle of unwanted orders being sent and billed to you. If you've been inundated with various mail order catalogs and circulars, this is a good time to escape them. Third class mail weighing less than sixteen ounces *won't* be forwarded to you unless the sender requests it.[4]

Your senior year is also a time to sift through your accumulated belongings and decide what to toss, what to give away, and what to take with you. Don't wait until the last week or two before graduation to do this; it can be an overwhelming task at a time when you have many other things you'd rather be doing. Start earlier in the year. Mark what stays and goes early, then wait to get rid of things closer to the end.

Some decisions can be tough. You may, for example, have grown to love the big old chair you got second hand during your sophomore year. It's the most comfortable chair you ever sat in, and it's got lots of great memories. It may, however, cost almost as much to get it moved to where you're going as it would to buy a new one in your new location. It might make more sense to sell it or to give it to a person or an organization that will make good use of it. Some seniors hand down their prized possessions to underclass students. Others have big tag sales and raise cash by selling what they're not going to take. If you're relocating to an area where other classmates are headed, one moving alternative is to share a rental van or truck. Compare rental, mileage, and insurance rates at several different companies; also find out how convenient it is to turn the vehicle in at the other end. Some employers offer a moving allowance. If you're planning to move more furniture than you can fit in your car, look into trailer, truck, or van rentals, or get estimates from moving companies. You'll need to do this well in advance to book a moving date. Another option is to get family or friends to help transport your belongings in several cars. If you're headed to an interesting area, that can be a good selling point to recruit help.

If you're going to be somewhere temporarily for the summer, you could store most of your belongings until you make a more permanent move. Weigh the pros and cons of your own situation based on expenses, convenience, and personal preference. If you're going to store things, get rid of what you don't plan to move with you before arranging and paying for storage. While the sorting process can be a pain, especially during your last few weeks on campus, you'll appreciate not having to do it on the other end, where you'll have as much, if not more, to do. You can find a self-storage facility in the yellow pages of the phone book. These facilities generally have monthly rates, and you retain the key to your rented space (but no, you can't live in your storage space!). Check out the security precautions and how easily you can gain access to your storage if you need to get to it before the end of the summer. Some places advertise twenty-four-hour access.

Some students enjoy the opportunity to start from scratch. They take off with a minimum of old belongings. You can mail or ship boxes to yourself. Books can be mailed at a relatively low book rate.

Making the Transition

I must admit I didn't like it at first. A big city, a huge grad school, lots of concrete, no ivy, and none of the New England charm I was used to. I was a small fish in a very large pond. I spent the

> first few weeks getting lost in subbasements and back hallways
> and going all over the city on the wrong busses.   —G.J.

Chapter 4 concentrates on the issue of looking for, and adapting to, various living and housing situations. The focus here is on the relocation transition—what to do right after you move.

Meeting People

First, tell yourself that beginnings are usually difficult, and resolve to give yourself time. It's a bit like breaking in a new pair of jeans after you've been wearing the same pair for a number of years. They were comfortable. They bent where you bent. It takes a while to work a new pair into the same kind of shape. They'll feel stiff and awkward at first, but the only way to get more comfortable in them is to wear them, even if the temptation is to shove them in the closet and put your old pair back on.

One graduate talks about needing a good six months to a year before she felt that she had made good ties. "You need to stay long enough to meet people," she said. The question becomes where and how to do that. If you're in a job or in graduate school, you have some built-in opportunities to initially meet people. I say initially because sometimes socializing just with the people you work with all day can turn out to be less than relaxing. One graduate describes how going out with people from work always turned into talking about the problems at work. "I didn't want to talk about work," he said. "I have a life." If, however, your office or graduate program sponsors activities like Friday afternoon bowling, aerobics, or other nonwork activities, this could give you a chance to interact with coworkers in an enjoyable, active setting, around a shared interest.

Even if you're not at a job or a graduate school that offers these opportunities, one of the best ways to meet people in a new location is to seek out groups or activities that interest you, such as community theater, volunteer work, or singing. Church, synagogue, or other religious-based activities; adult education courses; and sports activities were also cited by graduates as good ways to meet people they had something in common with. "You can't just sit home and eat popcorn and watch movies," says one.

If you're on a career track, local branches of professional organizations and your college alumni associations also offer the chance to meet people. Most cities also have publications or weekly newspapers that focus on cultural activities and group or organization meetings.

One of my biggest surprises after I graduated was finding that making friends was more complicated than it had been in college. Occasionally I would meet someone at work and get the feeling that we might become good friends. When this happened at college, the other person generally shared a similar student lifestyle and set of priorities. After college I found that new acquaintances were often juggling families, established circles of friends, and other responsibilities. They didn't always have the time it took to work at developing a friendship with me. We still had lunch together occasionally and had some good talks, but I realized that I needed to look elsewhere for those good friends I needed. I found them, but it took more time and effort.

Getting to Know the Area

You will also spend time getting to know your new location. Start with any materials you collected while looking at different areas during college. In many places you can buy large, detailed maps in local bookstores. For cities and suburban areas these may come in large magazine-sized booklets. These maps show every neighborhood and street and are great for planning how to get to places for the first time. They also show the locations of hospitals, schools, places of worship, shopping malls, libraries, post offices, parks, and so forth.

While exploring your new location, consider your own safety. Talk to neighbors and read the local newspaper for a few weeks to get an idea of where you shouldn't be wandering around alone. If you have no one to ask for advice, try calling the police station with some questions.

If you're moving to a city and will be using public transportation to get around, become familiar with your options. The yellow pages should list the number for the transit authority, and you can call for maps and schedules. In addition, schedules are often available in public libraries.

Two valuable resources in your new location are the yellow pages and the public library. When you arrange with the telephone company for service, your telephone books will be delivered shortly thereafter. Public libraries also have phone books from some large cities (and they may have computer files of phone listings for the whole United States), so you can get important numbers before you actually make your move. Federal, state, and local government offices and agencies are sometimes listed in a separate blue section of the yellow pages.

The public library is a gold mine. Find the nearest branch, get a card, and explore. The library provides information about jobs, housing, and activities. Federal and state government job listings are available. Local newspapers are received daily, and you can make use of the help wanted ads and the apartment ads as well as reading the local news. Libraries have community bulletin boards where you're likely to find posters advertising concerts, plays, meetings, lectures, and classes. Libraries also serve as distribution points for tax returns, adult education materials, local government publications, and some permits or licenses.

Some libraries have more advanced computer information files that include data bases of community associations and government services and organizations. With a click of the mouse you can call up information on subjects such as the arts, counseling, disability services, drug and alcohol abuse, education, the environment, employment and careers, health, law and legal aid, sports and recreation, and women. With a second click you can scroll through the specific agencies and find the address, phone number, contact person, description of the service offered, and other pertinent information to help you make the right connections. Other libraries will have this information in print, if they lack the on-line access.

Important Connections

> For some reason I always manage to find a mechanic, a dentist, and a gynecologist.   —C.C.

There are a number of connections you need to make in order to take care of your personal and property needs. In chapter 5 we'll talk specifically about financial issues and in chapter 6 about health care. As you seek professional services, you may encounter stereotypes or prejudices. Some business people initially look at recent graduates or those who look young as "kids" in a way that's synonymous with "irresponsible." So, make an extra effort to present yourself as a responsible adult when you approach these people.

> The stakes are too high for government to be a spectator sport.
> —Barbara Jordan[5]

Register to vote as soon as you're physically living in your new location. Contact your local board of elections or voter registration office for specific directions. There may be a voter registration form that you can pick up at a library or the post office. Once you fill out the form and send it in, the board of elections will return it to you at your address with information about your voting districts and polling place. If you check the Republican or Democratic party affiliation on your registration form, you'll be able to vote in that party's primary elections. In some states, if you register as an independent, you cannot vote in a specific party primary.

If you're moving to a new state and taking a car currently registered elsewhere, contact the motor vehicle department in your new state to get information about the laws there. Generally, you're expected to obtain a driver's license and title and register your car within a certain number of days after establishing residence in a new state. Call the motor vehicle department first, or stop by, to get a driver's handbook and information for new residents. Find out what tests (vision, written, road) you need to take to get a license in your new state. Many states waive the road test if you have a valid license from another state. Whether or not you have to take the written test, take time to study the driver's handbook in your new state. You'll need to know and get used to the driving laws—speed limits, whether you can make a right turn on red, and so on.[6] If you're moving to a state with traffic rotaries, get ready for a real challenge!

When you're ready to obtain your new license, bring your birth certificate, several other forms of identification, and documentation of any name change with you to the motor vehicle department. After you pass any tests needed (vision, written, road), you'll receive your new license and turn in your old one. Your previous driving history and record will be accessible to the motor vehicle department in your new state. License applications are checked with a National Driver Registry, and they will find out if yours has been revoked. Many states also belong to a National Driver License Compact, which shares information about drivers who have accumulated tickets anywhere in the country.[7]

To title and register your car in a new state, first have any state-required safety inspections done, and purchase state-required automobile liability insurance. Bring your safety inspection certificate with you, as well as your insurance policy (or a binder number for that policy if you haven't received it yet) and the company's and the agent's names. Also bring with you your out-of-state title as proof of ownership and fill out the application form for a title in your new state. If your out-of-state title is held by a bank or lending institution, request that they send the title to the motor vehicle department.

There will be fees for your license, for the title, and for the registration. These fees vary from state to state, so call ahead and find out how much you need to be prepared to pay in order to process all this material.[8] When you complete your registration process, you'll be issued license plates. Find out from your old insurance company where and how you should then return your old plates and cancel your old insurance.

If you're going to be in your new state for one year or less—attending grad school or temporarily employed—you may be able to keep your car registered in your home state and apply for a nonresident permit. This option is not available in all states, so contact the motor vehicle department where you're moving to get more information.[9]

Once the flurry of red tape is completed, you'll discover more subtle adjustments. These will help you make the emotional transition that is required to make your new location feel like home—like a pair of jeans that's comfortable and fits you well.

It took establishing personal landmarks to feel like I really belonged there and knew what I was doing—it was like: "This is where I do laundry, this is the fastest way to get to work, this is my favorite coffee shop, this is the theater with the best screen, this is the best restaurant in the neighborhood, this grocery store is better . . . if I know all these things, this must be my life."

—M.M.

F O U R

My Momma Told Me, You'd Better Shop Around: Room and Board

Luann, copyright © 1993 by Greg Evans. Reprinted with special permission of North America Syndicate.

Nothing prepares you for living on your own like living on your own. It's like needing to have experience to get a job, but needing a job to get that experience. If you've lived in a college residence hall or fraternity or sorority house, you may feel as if you've already lived on your own. To a degree you have, but there's still lots that is done for you on campus.

Heat, electricity, and meals are all provided. Campus security is available, often twenty-four hours a day. Residence hall rooms are furnished, and there are usually lounges, recreational facilities, and other services nearby. Some campuses have their own bus and escort services.

Starting Early

There are a variety of ways to get a taste of living on your own early. You may, for example, be a commuter rather than an on-campus resident. While some schools require that students live on campus for one or more years, others don't have strict residency requirements. If you commute from your parents' home, that won't really give you the experience of being on your own unless you are responsible for things like your own meals, bills, and chores. A year or a semester in your own or a shared apartment or house would provide the best practice. Some colleges have campus suites or apartments that would be a good compromise—retaining some of the trappings of campus life while adding some of the responsibilities of independent living.

Another step in this direction would be to spend a summer living on your own or with friends. This gives you a limited amount of time to learn what it takes to budget your money, be responsible for yourself, and be on your own before you have to do it for good. You can make mistakes on a smaller scale and learn from them.

Still another opportunity could come from house- or apartment-sitting for a professor or a friend who lives off campus. No matter how small the first step feels, take it. It's a bit like making progressively longer trips to the other side of your transition bridge, so that once you're over for good you feel more comfortable with this living on your own part of your new life.

> I don't think college (if you live on campus) really prepares you for living on your own. You just go to the dining hall. You don't even think about food. You do complain about it though. Then you go out there and find out, well, maybe it wasn't so bad after all.
> —M.L.

Part of living on your own involves shopping, cooking, and eating. Accumulate recipes and advice about preparing meals. If you visit friends for dinner and have a meal you really like, ask how to make it. Or, if you have some favorite meals at home, find out what it takes to prepare them. Most parents would be thrilled to be asked that question.

Senior Year

Generally, decisions about your postgraduation living situation will follow decisions about where you'll be and what you'll be doing. For example, you will need to wait to look for a place until you know where you're working or going to grad school. Or you may decide to move to a particular location and then look for a job there. There are several basic "givens" to consider in deciding on a living situation. First, it's important to feel safe and comfortable in your living environment. If you don't, it can affect your ability to function in other parts of your life. As one graduate says: "I've seen people self-destruct because they had a basement apartment." What's important is how you look at a situation. If you like the coziness of a basement apartment, great. If it makes you feel trapped, avoid living there, or find a way to look at the situation more positively:

- I'm saving enough money so I can treat myself to a concert ticket once a month in the winter and a major league baseball game once a month in the summer.
- I can plant some really nice flowers outside my bedroom window.
- I'll only be here one year, and then I'll be moving in with my boyfriend or girlfriend.

Second, live within your financial means, but also in a reasonable situation. Think about sharing a nicer apartment rather than living alone in a cheaper one that's in poor shape. Consider a less expensive apartment that's a greater distance from town but on the bus line rather than a more expensive place within walking distance of everything. Decisions about where and how to live involve much prioritizing and consideration of the trade-offs (I get this, but I don't have that).

For example, the first time I looked for an apartment was when I was moving to Philadelphia for graduate school. The nicest apartment I saw was one that I would have shared with a woman who was working full time. It was a twenty-minute train ride away from my school and in a high-rise with a resident population that was mostly over fifty years old. Great apartment, especially after seeing some awful places close to campus, but wrong for me in every other way. I kept looking.

Third, consider the commute as one factor when you narrow down your housing options. If you have to commit to a living situation before you have a job, try to live in an area that's accessible to a variety of work options. You may also make a temporary first move until your work or school plans come through. Most graduates I know keep their address books written in pencil for a few years, as their friends often move a couple of times before settling down.

Before you actually start to make decisions about your living situation, analyze your own lifestyle and personal needs. Identify your priorities before you have to make these decisions. That can speed the process along when you're actually looking for a place to live. Whenever I've had to look at potential places to live, I've been most successful using both my head and my gut instincts. When I looked at places, I would imagine myself coming home there at night, after an exhausting day. How would I feel walking in the door, and what would I need to do to try to relax? How would I feel having friends over? I tried to imagine a variety of situations and how I would deal with them in this apartment.

Exercise: What I Need

Imagine yourself walking into your own living situation—apartment, house, room. Let's say you'll be walking into this same place, day after day, for at least a year. Think about what's important to you in order to feel safe, comfortable, and energized.

1. Is it your own place, or are you sharing it with someone else? Who? _____

_____

_____

_____

2. What does your place look like (in a house, apartment complex, high-rise, low-rise, townhouse)? _____

_____

_____

_____

3. Who and what do you see when you look out your window(s)? What do you hear early in the morning and late at night? _____

_____

_____

_____

4. How many rooms are there, and what do they look like? _____

_____

_____

_____

5. What furniture is in your place, and what's it like? _____

_____

_____

_____

6. What's in your place that you know you could never live without (e.g., storage space for your bike, the bathtub, air conditioning)? _____

_____

_____

_____

7. How close can you park to your place, or how close to public transportation are you? _____

_____

_____

_____

8. How safe do you feel in your apartment and coming home there late at night, and why? _____

_____

_____

_____

9. What kind of setting/location/neighborhood are you in?

_____

_____

_____

10. What's the commute like to your job or school? In bad weather? During rush hour? _____

_____

_____

_____

11. How close are you to places where you can shop for what's important to you (e.g., groceries, videos, the Sunday newspaper)? _____

_____

_____

_____

12. How accessible are sources of entertainment and recreation (can you get to them fairly conveniently, or are they so hard to reach that you wouldn't take advantage of them)? _____

_____

_____

_____

13. What are your neighbors like (e.g., young people, families with small children, loud, friendly, everyone goes about their own business)? _____

_____

_____

_____

Once you've come up with your ideal responses, rank each of them into one of the three categories below.

1. Most important to you

_____

_____

_____

_____

_____

2. Would be nice, but not crucial

_____

_____

_____

_____

_____

3. Not very important

_____

_____

_____

_____

_____

If you focus your search using this information, you can more quickly eliminate options that don't meet your basic needs.

From a Distance

The next section of this chapter, "Making the Transition," goes into more detail about apartment hunting and moving in. You can, however, do some of the legwork during your senior year or the summer after graduation if you're able to visit your new location for a couple of days. Don't ever make a long-term commitment to a place sight unseen. The only exception, in a pinch, might be if a parent or a good friend you trust sees it and acts on your behalf. Even then, a temporary agreement would be safer than one requiring a lease. It can be a pain to move more than once, but that's certainly better than being stuck in an awful situation or losing money by having to break a legal agreement.

If you can take a couple of days to go to your new location to look for a place to live in person, that's the best approach. Do some preparation to make the most effective use of limited time there. For example, use the exercise described earlier in this chapter to focus on what's most important to you. Do some practice looking in your current area to find the kind of places you'd like to see, and get a feel for the kinds of questions you'd want to ask a landlord. Call the offices of the local newspaper in the area you'll be visiting. Ask if you can arrange to have some copies sent to you so you can look over the apartment ads.

The Apartment Relocation Council also publishes guidebooks for a number of cities throughout the country. Local issues are available free in places like supermarkets. You can also order guides for other parts of the country by phone (1-602-949-1900). Bear in mind, however, that the pictures and descriptions you see will probably all seem wonderful; that's the way they're supposed to seem. Check out *in person* any that interest you.

If you have any friends or relatives, or if your friends and relatives have any friends or relatives in the area where you're headed, get in touch with them. If you have a job already lined up, your employer may have some advice about areas for you to look for housing, or perhaps she or he can recommend a real estate agent. Your college alumni association may have publications that list alumni looking for room-mates or wishing to sublet apartments. Use these contacts to find out about general rental fees, utility costs, and particular neighborhoods and parts of town that would best meet your needs and be safe places for you to live. In addition to apartment listings, the local newspapers often give information like crime logs. You can also contact the police department to get information about the kinds of calls they get from the neighborhoods you're interested in. Once you've gathered this type of information, figure out a plan of action, make phone calls, and pound the pavement to check out the possibilities.

Real estate agents can be helpful if you have a limited amount of time to search on your own and don't know the new area well. If possible, call ahead and schedule an appointment for when you'll be visiting town. A real estate agent will ask you questions like how much you want to spend and what you're looking for, so you need to be prepared to tell them. They have listings of available places and information about them (sometimes pictures also), which can help you narrow down the places you want to see, and your agent can make the arrangements. She or he makes the calls and sets things up with the landlords or rental companies. Usually real estate agents' fees are paid by the landlord, but sometimes there will be a fee to you. Ask about that up front. Also be aware that some agents specialize in houses and others in apartments, so seek out one that's appropriate to your financial situation and the kind of place you're looking for. Some show places that will earn them a higher commission, so go with one who has been recommended by someone you trust. Real estate agents and landlords will also look for a record of responsibility on your part (for example, a job or a good credit history); be prepared to provide evidence of that.

If you're going to a graduate or professional school, the university where you're headed may have an office that lists housing options, as well as other students who want to share apartments. You can call ahead to ask for information. There may also be graduate student housing available on or near campus.

Making the Transition

Use a small notebook or index cards to jot down information about the living situations you see and your reactions and questions. As you're making final decisions, a friend, a parent, or an older brother or sister can be helpful as you consider your choices. If one of them is able to look with you, the additional point of view can be helpful. It will give you someone to talk to as you sort out your reactions. Friends or relatives who will try to impose their priorities and values on your choice, however, are best left out of the process.

Once you decide on a place, it can be a great relief to put a deposit down, sign the papers, and know you have a place to live that you're pleased with. Don't, however, take a place just to have the matter settled. It can sometimes be tempting to just put an end to a painful search by taking something—anything, especially if you've had a long, discouraging search. Don't make major decisions when you're feeling desperate. If you're not sure, don't commit yourself. If necessary, get something temporary while you continue to look. Friends and alumni from your college may be willing to put you up temporarily until you get your own place. You could also look for an inexpensive room at daily or weekly rates at the Y or a motel while you finish your apartment search. Some times of the year offer more choices as apartments open up. In college towns, for example, the end of the school year is a time when more may be available.

As soon as you have an address, arrange for telephone service. You can get your number and specify the day you want service connected. If your place already has jacks and you bring your own phone set, the process can be easily completed. Local phone service is provided by a basic carrier. If you expect to make only a limited number of brief calls from home, you might consider a lower-cost plan that charges you per call or by the length of the call. For a larger flat monthly fee, you can purchase an unlimited number of calls. Your phone company representative will explain your options when you call to set up your service, and the local phone book also explains them in writing.

Long distance service is another matter. You'll be inundated by options. AT&T, Sprint, MCI—all want your business, and they use TV commercial spokespeople like Candice Bergen, Sinbad, Whoopi Goldberg, and characters from *Friends, Picket Fences, Frasier,* and so forth to try to get it. Consider your own long distance calling patterns and needs, and compare what each has to offer. One strategy for comparing services is to submit a typical phone bill to each and ask what it would cost if you were their customer.[1]

First living situations after college graduation are often influenced by the reality of limited financial means. Even if you get a job with a decent salary, you may be paying off college loans. While buying a condominium or a house is a good investment, it is also a major commitment and expense. If you start your life after college with such a major purchase, you could be locking yourself into staying in an area before you know that that's where you want to stay, and into a financial commitment before you know that the job is one you will keep for the long term.

If you're moving away from home, you're best off finding a reasonable place to rent—perhaps even one that's furnished or that you can furnish inexpensively. As one person suggested, "Travel light and lean until you're sure you're staying somewhere. My first year I lived in an apartment with a lawnchair and a bed." If you have a pet you love and want to have live with you, you'll limit your living options. Many rentals don't allow pets, so leave the pet at home at least for now.

Furnishing Your Apartment

If you rent an unfurnished apartment, find a reasonable way to furnish it. Family and friends may have old pieces they're willing to donate. Recent graduates who are beginning to settle in more permanently may have first-apartment furniture they're replacing and would be willing to sell or give to you. Used furniture may not be your dream, but it can give you what you need for those first few years when other expenses are more pressing and when the last thing you need is a monthly furniture payment. Yard sales, moving sales, second hand stores, thrift shops, consignment shops, and ads in local *Pennysaver* publications or posted in supermarkets are all potential sources of used furniture. Some furniture can serve double duty. For example, I've used a trunk both to store things and as my coffee table. Perhaps your college or university periodically refurbishes some residence halls, pulling old furniture out of the inventory. The college may be willing to sell, at a cheap price, dressers, desks, beds, or bookcases that are no longer appropriate for the residence halls but may still be reasonable for you to use in an apartment for a year or two.

There are also inexpensive ways to get new furniture. My first bookshelves were cinderblocks and boards covered with orange burlap, and I kept them for many years. A door or a large board over a couple of two-drawer file cabinets can serve as a workable desk. There are also stores where you can buy unfinished furniture or furniture that you take with you and assemble yourself, saving on delivery and setup charges. If you decide to assemble something on your own, however, be sure you have the tools you need and that you can do it yourself or have help available. I once assembled a large round kitchen table upside down on a pedestal, then found I couldn't turn it right side up by myself!

When buying furniture, consider how it will be used and how practical and sturdy you need it to be. Have the measurements of your rooms with you when you go shopping. A piece so large that it gives you no space to move around is a mistake in your bedroom, for example, even if it looks great in the store.

You'll need at least something to sleep on. A good mattress and box springs are a wise investment, but they may initially be beyond your means. If you're planning to move again within the next few years, you also may not want to have to worry about moving a bed with you. A mattress on the floor or a futon can be a less expensive substitute. Linen for a double bed, mattress, or futon also tends to be less expensive than for a queen- or king-size bed. The local newspapers and Sunday newspaper inserts will let you know when sales are taking place. Be patient, and check prices of similar items at different stores. Some places claim they won't be undersold or will meet the lowest price you were quoted elsewhere. Take them up on the offer. This may not be as simple as it sounds, but it couldn't hurt to tell a salesperson if you were quoted less elsewhere. She or he may negotiate down or, at the worst, tell you to go back to the other place.

Types of Rental Options

By this time Mrs. Brown had reached the front of Kiswana's building and was checking the house number against a piece of paper in her hand. Before she went into the building she stood at the bottom of the stoop and carefully inspected the condition of the street and the adjoining property. Kiswana watched this meticulous inventory with growing annoyance but she involuntarily followed her mother's slowly rotating head, forcing herself to see her new neighborhood through the older woman's eyes.

—Gloria Naylor, *The Women of Brewster Place*[2]

When one graduate talked about her search to find a nice apartment, I asked her what a nice apartment was. "You know," she said, "one where your parents wouldn't die if they saw it." As you consider places to rent, start by figuring out how much you can reasonably afford to spend monthly. As a guideline, you should be able to cover your monthly rent and fixed expenses such as heat, electricity, phone, insurance, taxes, loans, and so forth with no more than two-thirds of your monthly take-home pay.[3] When rental rates are quoted to you, ask what is and isn't included in that monthly amount. What utilities will you have to pay in addition to rent? Heat? Hot water? Electricity? If you do have these additional costs, ask current tenants what their monthly bills average, bearing in mind that you may have different lifestyle needs than they do. Check also with the utility companies to see if they offer any budget plans or energy savings discount programs.

Rooms or apartments in houses are often less expensive than apartments in complexes. There may also be more room for negotiating rent, the security deposit, and the length of a lease. You may be living in part of a house with a family above or below you, so there could be some house rules or noise and privacy issues, or both, to consider. Ask to meet the people who already live there to get a sense of what it might be like to share these close quarters.

Apartments come in all types—one, two, or three bedrooms; townhouses, studios, and so forth. Generally, rents are higher in high-rise elevator buildings than in walk-ups or elevator buildings of three stories or less. Garden apartments or low-rise apartment complexes tend to be less expensive.[4] Complexes give you opportunities to meet new people, especially if there are facilities such as pools, tennis courts, clubhouses, laundry rooms, and playgrounds. As you look at apartment complexes, check out notices that are posted. These can give you an idea of what's going on and how the management communicates with tenants. Walk around. Are balconies cluttered, or do people seem to take care of their places? What condition are the grounds in? How about the unit you'd be renting? If you look at a place during the day, who's around? Try coming back in the evening or on the weekend to see what the environment is like when more residents are actually there.

Find out what maintenance services are available and how responsive they are to reports of problems. Are routine repairs handled promptly and efficiently? Can you call twenty-four hours a day for emergencies? Ask some current residents as well as the landlord or apartment manager.

If you're in a graduate or professional school program, some universities offer housing in graduate residence halls or apartments. This provides an opportunity for you to meet other students. It can also, however, feel like more of the residence hall life you graduated from. You may welcome this familiarity, or you may react as one graduate did: "Yuck, roommates again!"

I hold a strong conviction that everyone at some point in their lives should live by themselves if they can afford that luxury. I lived in a studio in Manhattan for a year and found it difficult at times, but overall rewarding for learning to depend only upon myself. It really gives you a lot of time to think, become truly self-reliant, and enjoy yourself, thereby building another dimension of your self-confidence. On the other hand, having a roommate at some point is also beneficial, but I think people tend to overlook the importance of being alone and coming to know oneself before trying to share oneself with others. This is the most valuable lesson I learned since graduating.   —R.C.

Leases

Leases are binding contracts between landlords and tenants. Once you sign a lease, you're committed for the period designated, and leases are difficult to get out of. Most leases run for a year. If you're not sure you'll be in your location for that long, or are hesitant to lock yourself in for a whole year at first, see if you can negotiate a shorter lease. It may not be possible, but you've got nothing to lose by trying. If you're working in a company that reserves the right to transfer you, ask the landlord to write into the lease that a job-mandated relocation is grounds for breaking the lease without a penalty. She or he may not agree to it, but it doesn't hurt to ask. Your lease should also indicate whether you can sublease the apartment to someone else, should you want or need to move.

The advantage of a lease is that it fixes your rent for the entire term of the lease; your landlord can't raise it on you during that time. Some agreements are done on a less formal basis, and either you or your landlord can terminate the arrangement at any time. While this gives you more flexibility to move at any time, it also allows your landlord to raise your rent at any time, or to kick you out arbitrarily.

Leases include information such as the beginning and ending dates of your tenancy, the amount of the rent payment and the date it is due each month (there is usually a penalty fee for late payments), and the responsibilities of both you and your landlord. Go over both the lease and the apartment before signing anything. If there is already any damage to the apartment, get in writing that it will be repaired before you move in, or at least make sure it's noted so that you won't be charged for that damage when you move out. Besides your first month's rent and any fees to the real estate agent, if you use one, you will have to put down a security deposit, usually a month's rent. When you eventually move out, the apartment will be inspected and you will receive back the security deposit minus the cost of any damage or excess cleaning needed. You can avoid this penalty by periodically doing those annoying cleaning jobs. For example, don't wait until the week you leave to clean your oven for the first time in three years. It won't be pretty!

Before you sign the lease, be sure you understand any rules or regulations you have to agree to. If you're not comfortable with any of them, and the landlord says they're negotiable, then get that in writing in the lease. If they're not negotiable, decide whether you can live with them or need to reconsider your decision to take the apartment.

Take time to read the lease carefully, especially the fine print. I once had a lease that would automatically renew itself for another year unless I notified my landlord thirty days in advance that I intended *not* to renew. Tricky. If I saw this clause today, I would try to get it changed so that wouldn't automatically happen.

Ask questions if you have them. It's your right to have someone with more experience (a parent, an older sister or brother, someone at your new place of employment or grad school) look over the lease before you sign. You may also want to check out the landlord or rental company. Most areas have fair housing organizations or lawyers who specialize in tenants' rights. Contact them to find out if your prospective landlord has a history of being uncooperative or unresponsive to tenants' needs. Remember that your lease should protect *both* you and your landlord. You have a right to get what you pay for. If you feel you're being treated unfairly, and your complaints are not being responded to, refer to one of the fair housing or tenants' rights resources.

Renter's Insurance

Renter's or tenant's insurance will cover your belongings, clothing, appliances, furniture, and so forth in case of fire or theft. It also covers your belongings when they're in your car or elsewhere. Renter's insurance (which is similar to condominium insurance, if you're going that route) is generally very reasonable, and the premium you pay will vary based on how many thousands of dollars of coverage you want. Some companies will give you a discount if you buy both automobile and renter's policies from them. If you're sharing an apartment with someone else, you should each have your belongings covered by your own policy.[5] If you accumulate additional belongings, you should update your coverage periodically.

You'll be asked to provide information for your renter's policy application. Your agent may know some of the facts, or you can ask your landlord for the information you need about

  construction or frame type (for example, wood, brick,
    aluminum siding)
  heat type (gas or electric)
  number of rooms
  how many family units are between each pair of fire
    walls
  where the fire retardant walls are located
  how far you are from the closest fire hydrant

Two or Three's Company

If you share an apartment with a roommate, you can save money and perhaps live in a nicer, safer, or larger place. Some graduates have also found that the money they saved this way helped them buy a car or pay off loans or save for their own condo or house sometime in the future. On the other hand, you may be tired of living with roommates, and it may be more important to you at this point to have space of your own, even if you have to cut back, for instance on what you spend for entertainment or books.

Graduate schools often have listings of other students looking for roommates or wanting to share apartments they're already in. Even if you're not in grad school, you may be able to go to a nearby college and look over the postings of people looking for roommates. Local newspapers often have similar listings. If you decide to share a place with someone else, approach this decision as carefully as you can. Two people going apartment hunting together and moving in together is one approach. Moving in to share an apartment with someone who is already living there involves different dynamics. Can you move in without feeling as if you're in someone else's apartment—where you always feel that it's more his or hers than yours? What do you need to do to work out an arrangement that feels equal?

As you consider apartment sharing situations, talk with potential roommates and assess the space you'd be sharing. Is the apartment large enough to comfortably house both of you? Is there room for privacy? Even if you plan on living with someone you already know, or a good friend, living together is tricky business. Some great friends stop being great friends once they have to handle the day-to-day business of living together. Discuss the usual kinds of questions (smoking/nonsmoking, night person/morning person, neat/sloppy, for example). Also consider other issues likely to surface when roommates aren't necessarily sharing the same student lifestyle. As one graduate notes, "Someone who works with people all day may want quiet time at night, and someone who crunches numbers all day may want company at night."

In addition to the personal issues, the logistics of sharing responsibilities create the need for other kinds of ground rules. For example, will one or both of you sign the lease? If only one of you does, she or he is responsible for the entire rent. How will you handle bills (rent, electricity, heat, telephone, and so forth)? Will one person's name be on the bill, or both? If your roommate's name is on the bill and she or he moves out, what will it cost to change the account over to your name? How will you divide food expenses? Will you each take care of your own? Will you split the cost of staples

Oh yeah sure . . . a real morning person!

and cleaning items that are cheaper in bulk? How will you share cleaning responsibilities—especially if you have different ideas about how clean you need things to be and how much time you have to work at it?

Dishes can become this paramount issue when you have a roommate. There are these dish wars. Whose turn is it to do them?

> How long can you leave them in the sink if it's his or her turn
> but she or he doesn't do them? Do you wash just yours and leave
> hers or his?   —M.L.

If your financial situations are very different (for example, one of you is a grad student on a small teaching assistant's stipend, and the other holds a comparatively well-paying computer analyst's job), that can also create tension around your shared style of living. Talk about the differences rather than ignoring them.

If sharing a place with one roommate saves money, obviously sharing a larger apartment or a house with several roommates can save more. Zoning laws, however, may limit the number of unrelated people who can live in one house. Check out the local laws where you intend to live. By sharing a house you can have some of the trappings of home— maybe a backyard, a big kitchen, or a basement. Some groups of college friends ease the transition to a new place by living together as a group. The trade-off is that the issues to be negotiated between a pair of roommates become increasingly complicated as you increase the number of housemates. The MTV show *The Real World* gives one view of this kind of group living situation.

Committed Relationships

Some graduates get married and share an apartment or other living situation with a wife or husband. Others are in committed relationships and choose to live together, considering themselves domestic partners. Discussions about finances and personal responsibilities are as important for couples as they are for arbitrary roommates—if not more important. If you're buying a condo or a house rather than renting, and you consider your relationship a partnership, consider putting the mortgage in both of your names. If you do that, each partner should take out a term life insurance policy that would provide the other with the funds to pay the deceased partner's share, should she or he die.[6]

Each partner contributes to the arrangement, whether in the form of money or of service (for example, work done in the home), and both types of contribution need to be valued. Make decisions together about how to manage money and divide expenses. One suggestion is for each partner to keep a separate bank account; when a shared expense, such as rent, is to be paid, each writes a check for his or her share. A second alternative is to keep a joint account for shared expenses and savings and separate accounts for individual expenses and savings.[7]

It's been said that money is one of the biggest sources of conflict for couples. While it's important that the basics be discussed, overemphasis on finances can overwhelm a relationship or serve as the vehicle for playing out other issues between the partners. A good example of this occurs in Amy Tan's novel *The Joy Luck Club,* when Lena confronts her husband Harold about the balance-sheet quality of their marriage.[8]

Going Home Again

The only problem that I encountered when I moved back home was being back under my parents' house rules. This was a big adjustment for me because for four whole years I came and went as I pleased, and I did whatever I wanted to do. Now that I was back under my parents' roof, I could not stay out as late as I could when I was away at school. This took some getting used to, but I was able to adjust. Furthermore, my parents made some adjustments as well. They realized that I was older, and that I was not the same person that I was four years ago when I left for college. They also realized that I was used to having my freedom and independence. Therefore, my parents and I were able to compromise.   —B.T.

More college graduates seem to be returning home, at least partly because of the financial pressures of independent living. The return home requires patience and adjustment on the part of both graduate and parents. One graduate was appalled when, after four years away at college and one year on his own abroad, he returned home, went out to eat with his parents, and found his mother starting to read to him from the menu. Another found herself falling into old patterns in which she felt as if she was one of the kids again. "I had to negotiate and bargain about which seat I'd get at the dinner table," she said. "And when we'd all go somewhere in the car, I'd still have to fight with my brother about who'd have to sit in the middle."

It is the responsibility of both the graduate and the parents to negotiate new ground rules. It won't necessarily be easy, but it will reflect the changes in your relationship. Your parents need to get used to seeing you more as an adult; you, in turn, need to understand that your return may cause some readjustment in their lives also. Discuss ground rules before you make a decision about returning home. Talk honestly about what you each need from one another to make it work. If the situation doesn't look workable, explore other alternatives, such as your parents lending you money if you can't afford the initial costs of getting your own place, or living with a brother or sister instead.

While it helps to have the overhead taken care of while you concentrate on beginning your career, repaying loans, and so forth, it's important to establish a responsible pattern as an adult in preparation for the time when you go out on your own. Pay your parents some room and board, and have some specific bills (for example, your own phone) that are in your own name and that you are responsible for paying regularly. Your parents may feel awkward having you pay some expenses. Explain to them why it's important for you to demonstrate a record of financial responsibility.

This baby lived with his parents until he was twenty-four years old. It was a good life: food was free, there was hot and cold running water, and my laundry was done—eventually. It took a while to have my laundry done because my hamper was the floor of my room. I learned what many young men have learned: if you leave your clothes on the floor of your room long enough, you can wait your mother out. Sooner or later, she will pick them up and wash them for you. The price you pay will merely be her noisy disgust: "All these stinking moldy clothes . . . just a disgrace . . . at twenty-four . . . he must think I'm his slave . . . he must think I want to start some kind of *collection* of rotting clothes." Fathers, however, are a little tougher about such earthy living. My father set my clothes on fire.

　　　　　　　—Bill Cosby, "Look Homeward, Sponger" [9]

You may also have to battle a tendency to see returning home as going back to an earlier way of life. It's not. In addition to establishing some financial independence, take responsibility for some of your own chores and personal care needs—including some cooking and cleaning. For example, though it may be easier to leave your laundry for someone else to do, learn how to do it yourself.

If you've already been doing your own laundry in college, you already know to follow the instructions on the washer and dryer lids and to wash dark colored and light colored clothes in separate loads. Use cold water to keep the color of dark clothes from running. You can avoid the problem of soap clumping together (instead of dissolving as it should) by putting the appropriate amount of detergent on the bottom of the washer, starting it so the water starts to fill, *then* adding your clothes. It's also worth a little extra time to dry most clothing at a lower temperature setting to minimize shrinkage. Don't leave clothes sitting in the dryer after it stops; they'll get very wrinkled. If this happens, sometimes running them through for another ten minutes of drying time helps to get rid of the wrinkles.

The clothes you'll need to wear (and launder) when you enter the workforce will be different from your college wardrobe. The labels inside clothing items tell you how to best care for and clean them. "Dry clean only" labels indicate that you need to take the garment to a dry cleaner rather than being able to just toss it in the washer and dryer yourself.

Natural fibers such as cotton, silk, and wool are most comfortable to wear in any climate; they adjust to your body temperature. They are, however, less practical for cleaning. One hundred percent cotton shirts, for example, need to be ironed after you wash and dry them. Polyester, or permanent press clothing, is easier to wash and dry and doesn't wrinkle as much or require ironing. If you don't mind ironing, you may opt for the more comfortable cotton. If time is of the essence, you may prefer the more convenient polyester.

Food, Glorious Food

> When I was in grad school I lived five blocks away from a Baskin Robbins and I would just walk down the street and buy a pint of ice cream. That would be my meal. And I thought it would be OK because hey, I got my exercise—I walked to Baskin Robbins and back.   —C.V.

For some of you, the opportunity to shop for, cook, and eat what you want may feel like a great gift. No more traveling through a cafeteria line having to decide between mystery meat and a vegetarian surprise. Say good-bye to those little individual cereal boxes. As much as you may have complained about the repetitious dining hall selections, however, you could always get a balanced meal if you wanted it. The challenge now is how to eat within your financial means nutritiously and enjoyably.

Some graduates have developed shopping into a fine art. Others play it by ear and wind up buying too much, too little, or food they never eat. The following suggestions are guidelines for you to consider as you become a regular shopper. We each develop our own system for shopping. You'll decide for yourself, too.

If there are some items you like always to have in the house (for example, milk, juice, oranges, ketchup, spaghetti), keep a list of what you're running low on so you can replace things before you run out. This can also help you avoid standing in the supermarket aisle trying to remember whether you do or don't need mustard, then buying it and discovering you already had two unopened jars at home. If you're planning a particular meal, write down all the ingredients you'll need, check to see which you already have at home, and put on your shopping list only what you actually need to buy.

> At first it annoyed me to think about every purchase, but then it became a way of life.   —M.J.

If you're on a tight budget, look for sale items and clip coupons from the newspapers. Coupons for items on sale (especially if you shop at a store that doubles coupons) can maximize your savings. Be careful to check the cost of non-coupon brands also. Sometimes your coupon "bargain" is still more expensive than another comparable brand at regular price. Generic or store brands tend to be cheaper than name brands, and the difference in taste and quality is often minimal. Do some taste testing and try some of the generic brands. If you like one, you can substitute it for the more expensive item.

If there's a special sale on something you use regularly, stock up on it. Some items can be bought more cheaply in bulk, and you can cook and freeze what you want to save. Only buy in bulk, though, if it's something you'll eat and if it has a long enough shelf life to give you time to finish it. A bargain isn't much of a bargain if it spoils and you wind up throwing it away. If you tend to freeze a lot of food, new or left over, keep a list of what's in your freezer and when you froze it, so you can eat older food before it gets old enough to vote!

There are different points of view about comparison shopping. Some people like to go to different stores for different things—to a food warehouse or coop for bulk items, to a farmer's market for fresh fruits and vegetables, to one store for chicken and fish, and to another for everything else. A few people like to grow their own vegetables, herbs, and spices in their gardens. Others see comparison shopping as more hassle than it's worth to them, and they pick the store that's closest, or that they like best. Some occasionally do some comparison of prices but don't get overly concerned about it.

Small convenience stores tend to be more expensive than larger chain supermarkets. Manufacturers' outlets and thrift stores with "day olds" of, for example, one particular bakery brand, can offer good bargains.[10] Large membership warehouses offer some of the lowest prices, although they don't always give the same degree of service as supermarkets. You may need to belong to a particular group (for example, a community association or a credit union) to qualify for membership, and you may also have to buy in larger quantities than you can use.[11]

The same food can be bought in a number of forms and variations. For example, green beans may be fresh, frozen canned, or dried. Usually, canned and frozen are less expensive except when fresh are in season. Olives, for another example, are sold whole, sliced, chopped, and pitted. Generally, chopped and crushed are less expensive. Fresh fruits and vegetables from bins are better choices than those that are prepackaged because the packaging can make it hard to see cracks or decayed areas. Be sure to examine what you're buying.[12]

Calculate the unit prices of similar items. Some stores are considerate enough to post the unit prices—by the pound or by the ounce—clearly on the shelves. If the place you shop doesn't do this, you can easily calculate the unit price yourself if you carry a pocket calculator with you. Divide the cost of the item by the number of ounces contained. This will give you the price per ounce, and you can compare unit prices to get your best buy.[13] For example, a forty-ounce jar of peanut butter for $6.19 costs fifteen cents an ounce and is cheaper than an eighteen-ounce jar at $2.99, which ends up costing you seventeen cents an ounce; the eighteen-ounce jar, in turn, is cheaper than a twelve-ounce jar at $2.29, which costs nineteen cents an ounce. Remember, though, a larger yet cheaper size that will sit on the shelf and spoil before you finish it isn't really cheaper at all.

A few words about those freshness dates stamped on food packages. The "use by" date means the item isn't at peak freshness after this date (but it won't hurt you!). "Sell by" indicates the last date it can be sold in the store. Most items are usable about a week beyond this date. I know that I'm not the only one in the supermarket who stands by the milk cartons searching for the one with the most distant "sell by" date on it. The "expiration date" indicates the last date an item should be used. If it's been in your refrigerator past that date, toss it.[14]

One other piece of advice—nonfood items such as toothpaste, detergent, and trash can liners are generally more expensive in grocery stores than they are in discount stores. Plan periodic trips to a discount store to take care of these nonfood purchases. Keep track of your supplies so you don't run out and have to spend more at a grocery store because you're in a bind.[15]

Don't Worry, Be Healthy

If we had a menu for the way we now think about food, it would look like a prescription pad. Any day now, I expect even the supermarkets to arrange their aisles: complex carbohydrates to the right, simple to the left. I cannot date the precise moment when we began to think of food as medicine. I know for sure that the nutrition I learned in school was as circumscribed as the four basic food groups. I got the general idea that as long as there were different-colored foods on our plates, we were okay.
—Ellen Goodman, "Eating Our Medicine"[16]

I used to think I didn't have time to worry about shopping and eating nutritiously. Once my rising cholesterol level scared me, however, I learned that it really took more will power than time. Get used to reading the labels on the food you're buying. The list of ingredients is arranged in decreasing order of quantity. If you see, for example, that sugar and some unpronounceable chemical are the first two ingredients listed, put it back on the shelf and move on. Recent federal laws have mandated that most foods in the grocery store now have, in addition to an ingredient list, a nutrition facts label. Look over this information before putting a package into your grocery cart.

Nutrition Facts

Serving Size ¹/₂ cup (114g)
Servings Per Container 4

Amount Per Serving

Calories 90   Calories from Fat 30

% **Daily Value***

Total Fat 3g	**5**%
Saturated Fat 0g	**0**%
Cholesterol 0mg	**0**%
Sodium 300mg	**13**%
Total Carbohydrate 13g	**4**%
Dietary Fiber 3g	**12**%
Sugars 3g	
Protein 3g	

Vitamin A	80%	• Vitamin C	60%
Calcium	4%	• Iron	4%

* Percent Daily Values are based on a 2,000
calorie diet. Your daily values may be higher or
lower depending on your calorie needs:

	Calories	2,000	2,500
Total Fat	Less than	65g	80g
Sat Fat	Less than	20g	25g
Cholesterol	Less than	300mg	300mg
Sodium	Less than	2,400mg	2,400mg
Total Carbohydrate		300g	375g
Fiber		25g	30g

Calories per gram:
Fat 9   •   Carbohydrate 4   •   Protein 4

The percentages of daily values on the label are based on people who need two thousand or twenty-five hundred calories each day. Try to limit the number of calories that come from fat, and choose foods with a larger difference between the total number of calories and the number from fat. Both of these figures will be listed directly under the amount per serving on the label. Choose foods with a low percentage of daily value (the far right column on the label) of fat, saturated fat, cholesterol, and sodium. Saturated fat contributes the most to raising blood cholesterol, so look for a low percentage of it.

Reduce your total fat intake to between 20 percent and 30 percent of your total calorie count. To stay within this range, try not to exceed sixty-six grams of fat intake per day. When looking at food nutrition labels, a listing of about three grams of fat for every one hundred calories is a good guideline to follow.[17]

Too much cholesterol can lead to heart disease. Try to eat less than 300 mg each day. Sodium, or salt, contributes to high blood pressure in some people. For total carbohydrate, dietary fiber, vitamins, and minerals, the goal is to reach 100 percent of each every day.[18] As an overall rule of thumb, eat more fruits and vegetables (strive for five a day), include plenty of fiber, and limit your fat intake, especially saturated fats.

You don't necessarily have to walk around calculating the percentages of everything you buy and eat. It is helpful, however, to get into the habit of buying and keeping on your shelves foods that are more healthful. Understand the basic nutritional information so you can scan a label and get a general sense of whether that item is, on balance, more healthful or less.

Cooking and Eating

> This was hard in the beginning because I had never cooked in my whole life and I love to eat. Because my mother is a phenomenal cook who doesn't follow recipes, I would try to picture what she did and imitate. Somehow it just didn't come out the same. In the first few years, shopping for food, cooking, eating, and cleaning would be an entire evening's activity. Slowly, over time, I've managed to actually pick up a few key tips and hints to speed up the process and come out with a real meal!   —R.C.

"I hope I never see an Oodles of Noodles again in my life," sighed one graduate when we started to talk about her early culinary experiences. It may take some effort and creativity, but you can certainly develop your cooking skills and repertoire. Ask your relatives who cook to give you recipes for dishes you remember liking best. Also, a cookbook would make a nice graduation present, if someone asks. Start with one that's pretty basic, unless you're already an experienced cook. If you'll be on your own, you may want a cookbook that emphasizes cooking for one or two. Avoid recipes with exotic ingredients you'll have to buy, use once, and never use again. If you're working long hours or in school all day, look for recipes that don't take a long time to prepare. As you try out new recipes, write some reactions in the cookbook ("looks good, tastes lousy," "great but makes enough for an army—cut ingredients in half next time").

Post-it notes on the page are a good alternative if you hate to write in books.

Cooking and eating with friends and new acquaintances can be a good social activity. Try pot luck dinners, for which everyone brings one dish, or perhaps once a month or so several of you could get together to prepare and eat a meal. Some people like to cook but don't have time during the week. You can cook a pot of chili, for example, on a weekend, eat some that night, and freeze portions to use in the week or two ahead. A group of friends can individually cook large amounts of different meals, divide them up into serving-size portions to freeze, and exchange those portions with one another. Then, instead of eating chili for two weeks, you can enjoy a greater variety of meals (assuming your friends are decent cooks!).

Shake, Rattle, and Roll

If you're starting out in your first apartment, you'll need some basic equipment for your kitchen. Of course, your own lifestyle and eating preferences will influence what you need, or what you need *first*, but consider these suggestions.[19]

Good knives are a *must*. They should be high-carbon stainless steel and should be kept in a rack, not in a drawer. Sharpen them periodically. Different types of knives serve different purposes. A chef's knife with a three-to four-inch blade is good for mincing herbs and peeling; one with a six- to eight-inch blade is best for chopping most vegetables; and a ten- to twelve-inch blade is used for slicing through large foods such as eggplant. A ten- to twelve-inch serrated knife is most effective for slicing bread, and a shorter serrated knife is best for slicing soft fruits such as tomatoes.

If you're going to be doing any cooking on top of your stove, you'll need pots and pans. Avoid wooden or plastic handles. Frying pans should have nonstick linings. A good variety would include a large pot with a lid (for cooking foods such as spaghetti or corn on the cob), a ten-inch nonstick frying pan with a lid, and various sizes of saucepans with lids. You can often find packaged sets of pots and pans that provide a basic combination of sizes.

Depending on your cooking and eating priorities, other basic equipment for your first kitchen could include

wooden spoons
plastic spoons and spatulas
a soup ladle
tongs (for grasping food too hot or cold to touch)
a vegetable peeler
a can opener
a bottle opener
measuring cups
measuring spoons
a cheese grater
a strainer
a colander
a big wooden salad bowl
a set of stainless steel mixing bowls
a baking sheet (insulated or air cushioned)
one or more oven-proof casserole dishes with lids
a loaf pan

glass baking dishes

a pizza pan

a plastic cutting board

plastic freezer containers that you can also use in the
microwave

a plastic pitcher (for frozen juice)

a teakettle

pot holders (to protect your hands from hot things)

kitchen towels

a fire extinguisher (just in case!)

Some machines or small appliances can be helpful if you intend to use them often—a food processor, a vegetable steamer, a small hand mixer. A microwave is helpful for preparing meals quickly after a hard day's work.

You'll also need utensils, dishes, and glasses. These don't have to be fancy or expensive, and you don't need service for twelve. They don't even have to match. Often family members have extras that they're happy to give you. Yard sales, restaurant supply stores, discount stores, and promotional give-aways such as a free Batman glass with a large soda, are less expensive sources. You also don't have to get everything right away. As you manage your own cooking, you'll discover what you need. Don't think your first kitchen has to rival Julia Child's; you could wind up with lots of equipment you'll never use.

Eating Out

It can feel like hard work to cook for yourself if you're not used to it. You also have to work harder at eating well when you're working at a job and you're on your own. It's easier to eat out, but that's also infinitely more expensive. Pack your own lunch; it's a frugal alternative to eating lunch out every day. Check what resources (for example, refrigerator, microwave) are available for you to use at work or school, and plan what you can most effectively bring with you for meals.

There are ways to more reasonably include some eating out-opportunities. When I was in graduate school, my university newspaper would publish a supplement each fall listing all the restaurant specials—dollar nights, all-you-can-eat buffets, and so forth. This helped us decide which night to go where for what when we were low on funds (pasta night at one place on Mondays, half price pizzas at another on Wednesdays, happy hour with free appetizers at still another on Fridays). Doggie bags can also stretch a lunch out of last night's restaurant dinner out. Early bird specials (before 5:00 p.m. or so) are also a good deal, and if you choose lunch out over dinner out, you'll find you can get the same food at the lower lunch prices.[20] Several graduates suggest volunteering for graduate school or job meetings or functions that serve breakfast, lunch, or dinner to those who attend. One graduate proudly proclaimed, "I never say no to free food!"

FIVE

Twist and Shout: Finances

The key to successful financial management is to develop good habits and develop them early. Besides setting a pattern for later, the foundation you build, or the hole you dig, can influence your situation throughout much of your life. For example, if you start saving a specific amount every month starting in your twenties, you will benefit from that foundation when you're ready to retire. On the other hand, piling up large credit card bills early on will saddle you with a debt with interest that continues to dig the hole deeper every month — one that may take many years to finally pay off.

Starting Early

Throughout your earlier years in college, take steps to be responsible for at least some of your own financial management. You could, for example, work during the summers or part time during the school year, or both. Have your own savings and checking accounts and keep track of them. If your parents pay for, or help pay for, your education, ask them to specify what they will do (for example, pay tuition bills or deposit a monthly allowance into your account) rather than leaving matters open-ended so that you just call home whenever you run out of money. Parents who are, and can afford to be, generous bottomless pits won't necessarily be helping you learn what it means to be financially responsible in a world where you often have to make choices. One graduate, for example, describes how she began to learn about being financially responsible one summer. Her parents paid the rent for the summer while she worked and was responsible for all her other expenses. She was able to learn from her mistakes in a more short-term situation. This helped her approach her postgraduation life with more knowledge and experience.

Your college or community may offer educational opportunities for you to learn about financial issues. These can range from undergraduate academic electives in economics, business, and accounting to local adult education courses on taxes, law, financial management, and retirement planning. Magazines (for example, *Money* and *Cosmopolitan*) and newspapers generally have articles and columns about financial planning. Read them periodically to begin to get a feel for the terminology and the issues. If you know professors or friends of your parents or parents of your friends who are in fields like insurance, banking, or investment counseling, ask questions about what you're reading or want to understand better. Morning television programs such as *Today, Good Morning America,* and *This Morning* often have segments and interviews with experts on these topics.

If you're interested in computers, financial management software packages, such as *Quicken,* can help you organize and keep track of your finances. Budget spreadsheet programs are offered by packages such as *Lotus 1-2-3, Quattro Pro,* and *Excel.*[1] The computing facilities at your college may give you a chance to introduce yourself to programs such as these before deciding whether they will be helpful for you.

> Get a credit card before you graduate, but do not be lured into thinking that you have more money than you have—try to pay off your entire balance every month. Your future financial dealings will involve scrutiny of your credit history—if you mess up your credit now you may have trouble buying a house ten years from now. Credit cards are very easy to obtain, but that doesn't mean they should be taken lightly. I've been amazed to see my friends that are very smart about everything else get into real trouble over credit cards.   —M.M.

These early college years are also a time to begin to develop a good credit history. College students are often given the opportunity to apply for credit cards without the usual annual fee. Establish a good credit history by using the card wisely—charging small amounts at a time and paying off your bill promptly and in full each month. Establish a record as a good customer. This will result in your credit line increasing and your having greater credit power later on when you may need it to buy a car or qualify for a mortgage loan.

Maintain a good driving record. Accidents, or more than one ticket, can escalate your insurance rate or even make you uninsurable when you look for automobile insurance on your own. Also, a history of auto insurance coverage as part of your parents' policy can enable you to get your own coverage in a lower risk (and less expensive) category than if your first application for automobile insurance is on your own for your own car.

Finally, use campus jobs and student activity and organization opportunities to develop your financial knowledge and experience. Student activities, such as successfully managing an organization budget, can prepare you for larger budget responsibilities in the workplace. Serve as treasurer of a club or organization, or work in an office such as financial aid or the controllers office. These experiences will give you exposure to people who can teach you a lot about financial management. A responsible work record and credible references will also work for you when you need them in the future.

Senior Year

If you haven't already begun acting on the suggestions offered in the previous section, it's not too late to start. Also find out what the financial implications are when your status shifts out of the student category. For example, if you have a free or low-fee student bank account and are staying in the same area after you graduate, can you retain the account at the same rate? If you haven't yet obtained a credit card at a low fee or no fee, consider it now, especially if your future plans are uncertain. Some companies will offer a card to a college student, but they wouldn't issue one to that same person as an unemployed graduate just two months later.

If you're considering graduate or professional school, look into costs and financial aid and grants available to you (see also chapter 7). Talk with your financial aid office about additional loans you might need if you continue on directly. Weigh the pros and cons of working for a while before you begin a graduate program that requires more loans.

Budgeting is an important skill to learn in college, even though your income and expenses will probably be very different once you're working. You should get used to the general budget process before you graduate. If you don't currently manage all your finances, the reality of what that involves could come as a shock. One episode of Bill Cosby's TV show demonstrated this with a very concrete example. The son in the show, Theo, had decided to drop out of high school and live on his own. His father was determined to show Theo what that would mean, using Monopoly money as a prop. He handed his son the amount that Theo thought he'd be earning each month. Then he started taking the Monopoly money away—for taxes, rent, utilities, phone, transportation, food, entertainment, and so on. Theo was empty-handed in no time. The point was made.

Take some time now to look at how much you spend and what you spend it on. Which of these expenses are necessities in college but probably won't be after you graduate? Which aren't really necessities at all? Once you graduate and your lifestyle changes, what other changes do you anticipate (a larger income, higher living expenses, commuting expenses, a new wardrobe for work)?

Making the Transition

Managing Your Budget and Bills

> To be independent while remaining comfortable and safe, I felt it was important to live practically and frugally. I stayed away from any major purchases both to save money and to remain unencumbered so I wouldn't be tied down if I needed to move again. Despite all my efforts I still hit a period during which I felt as if I was completely unable to keep up with my bills. I remember calling home and crying about how I felt as if I was drowning in a sea of debt and couldn't manage. I expected to get sympathy, but in my mother's strong-willed fashion she delivered a stern comparison of how she emigrated to America all on her own slightly older than I was and fended for herself. How could her daughter not be able to manage only four hours away from home? I remember how her words instantly humbled me and comforted me by illustrating how comfortable my situation really was relative to so many others. The next month I was fine again.   —R.C.

Once you know what you'll be doing after graduation, you can begin to realistically consider your budget. Budgeting may feel like a pain, but it can help you to avoid overspending on less important items and keep you from ignoring longer-term goals that require early planning.[2]

Start with your monthly income. How much will you take home each month (your net pay after taxes and payroll deductions)? Keep your paycheck stubs. They provide important information about specific payroll deductions such as social security and federal and state taxes withheld. Will you have any other regular monthly income—savings account interest, or an allowance? Next, enumerate your fixed monthly expenses—rent, electricity, phone, food, car payments and upkeep or carfare, student loan payments, support for family members, and so forth.

Although it's not necessarily a money saving measure, you can level your utility bills throughout the year to avoid extremely high heating or air conditioning bills that put a strain on your monthly budget. Check with your utility companies about the availability of this kind of plan.[3]

There are a number of fixed expenses that you pay yearly or semiannually or quarterly—renter's insurance, car insurance, health insurance if it's not one of your job benefits, medical costs. Translate these into monthly costs by dividing, for instance, an annual charge by twelve or a quarterly charge by three. Fixed expenses should total no more than two-thirds of your monthly take-home pay. If you can keep the total lower than that, it's even better.[4]

Try to build up an emergency savings fund equal to one to three or even six months of your regular salary. This will tide you over in the event of sudden additional expenses such as major car repairs, a family emergency, or being left to pay the entire rent on an apartment if your roommate leaves unexpectedly, and it may allow you to avoid borrowing the money at high interest rates.[5]

Develop an organized approach to paying your bills. Have a specific place where you keep them after they arrive, and plan to pay them shortly before they're due, not as soon as you receive them and definitely not late. If you have the choice of paying a bill by credit card rather than by check, using the card will buy you some additional time. It takes a credit card transaction longer to clear your bank and be deducted from your account than it will take your check to do the same thing. This will let your money remain a bit longer in a savings or interest-bearing checking account if you have one.[6]

Plan to pay your bills at the same time each month. Many recent graduates in their first jobs pay their monthly bills with their regular paychecks. This requires organization. When do you receive your paycheck and how frequently? Look at when your regular bills are due. Each will specify a due date, after which you'll pay a late charge. My bills, for example, are due as follows.

rent	first of the month
gas and electric	first of the month
credit card	21st of the month
phone	first of the month
cable	19th of the month

My bill paying method is to hold my rent, phone, and gas and electric bills when they arrive and pay them as soon as I receive my monthly check on the twenty-fifth. I also sit down on the fifteenth day of every month to pay my cable and VISA bills so they're received by their due dates. This is actually a good schedule for someone who gets paid every two weeks. She or he could then pay three of the bills from the first check each month and the other two from the second. As I'm on a once-a-month pay schedule, I simply have to adapt. Another alternative would be for me to contact VISA and the cable company to ask whether they could change my monthly due date to accommodate my pay schedule. If they did, I could do all my check writing at one time each month.[7]

There's one bill you won't receive in the mail that should nonetheless be paid each month. This is a bill you pay to yourself—to your savings. Some suggest that 10 percent of your gross income (before taxes and deductions) is a goal to aim for. This could be a stretch for a recent graduate, especially if you have debts to pay off such as student loans. Pay off your debts, especially those with large interest charges. This should be a priority. You should still try to save something consistently each month, no matter how small the amount. You can increase the amount you save as your circumstances allow.[8] Another way to feed your savings account is to have your paycheck deposited into your savings account, where it earns interest, rather than into your checking account, where it generally doesn't. You could then transfer from savings to checking only the amount you know you'll need for your monthly expenses and leave the rest where it can earn some interest for you.[9]

Your monthly income minus your monthly fixed expenses can give you an idea of how much in discretionary funds you will have left—money to spend or save as you see fit. Your first regular full-time job salary may feel like an incredible amount of money. The temptation is often to spend it on things you've always wanted to get. Be patient. Consider what you really need now and what can wait a while.

Another helpful approach to budgeting is to look at what

you actually do spend money on. This can be done by keeping track of your expenses over the course of several months. Your checkbook register and credit card statements document your spending. Keep an ongoing written record of expenses that don't show up on either but are part of your spending pattern (the newspaper, carfare, snacks at work). Even though it can feel like a pain, keep track of everything you spend over a several-month period. After this period, look back over your monthly expenditures. Are some items eating up more than they should? If any are greater than 15 percent of your take-home pay, that's a sign to start cutting back on them.[10] Here is where you can begin to set up limits on spending in some categories.

If you move home directly after graduation, you should still begin to take responsibility for managing your finances, as a graduate describes below.

> Although I moved back home, I gave my parents money for rent, and I began paying my own car insurance, health insurance, and life insurance, along with all of the other expenses that I incurred. This was a big adaptation because when I was in school, my parents took care of all my expenses. Now that I am out of school, I have to pay my own expenses. Although this took some getting used to, it has taught me responsibility in spending and managing money.   —B.T.

Cutting Expenses

There are creative ways to cut costs without totally eliminating items. For example, in addition to books, public libraries have magazines and newspapers. It may be more convenient to get them delivered to your house or to pick up copies at the store, but you can read magazines and newspapers for free at the library. Videotapes can be borrowed from the library for less than it costs to rent them at a video store, and tapes and CDs can also be borrowed. Your library may also sell some used books, tapes, and CDs.

Look for dollar movie theaters, or go to movie matinees or cheaper twilight shows. You can save a few dollars if you go to the earlier show and have a bite to eat afterward rather than going to eat first and then to see the same movie at night for several dollars more. You can see plays or concerts free by ushering, and preview performances of plays are often less expensive. Take advantage of low-cost entertainment if you live near a college or university campus. Some museums also have one day a week when admission is free or on a pay-as-you-can basis. If you're a graduate student or even taking just one course at a local college, get a student ID. That card can often get you lower-priced entry to a variety of events and activities both on the campus and in the community.

Look at what you think are some of your fixed expenses. There may be ways to save there, too. Utility companies have energy savings programs that can also save you money. Ask your local utility companies about them. Take advantage of differing electric rates at different times of the day. Shift some of your power usage to off-peak hours when it will cost you less. For example, shower, use the dishwasher, do laundry, and so forth. later at night or on weekends when the cost of power is least expensive.[11] Telephone rates vary at different times of the day. Check with both your local and your long distance carrier for accurate information to help you save the most on your phone use.

Learn basic home maintenance information such as how to reset a circuit breaker, how to unclog a stopped-up toilet, and how to fix a leaky faucet. If you're able to take care of these types of problems yourself, you'll save the expense of having to call in a plumber or an electrician.

If you subscribe to cable TV, take a good look at your real needs and actual use. For example, do you pay for premium channels to see recent movies while also renting videos to play on a VCR? The question to ask yourself about many expenses is, Do I really *need* this, or is it something I just want? Careful choices now may save you money that can contribute to some necessities and long-term wants.

Record Keeping and Taxes

> Someone in the show I was in had mentioned that you had to save receipts and take them to an accountant before April 15. I kept them all in a big shoebox and brought them to an accountant on the fourteenth. They were in no particular order. I just dumped them on the accountant's desk and expected him to do something magical.
>
> —Rita Rudner, "If I Live in a Fantasy World, Why Do I Have to Pay Taxes?" [12]

Try an accordion file or a set of file folders rather than a shoe box or shopping bag! For each year (January through December, not the school year calendar you may be used to) file your different types of bills (for example, phone, credit card, loans, medical) in separate pockets. As a rule of thumb, keep all your records—paid bills, receipts, canceled checks, and so forth—for three years, starting a new accordion file or set of folders each January. Also retain your tax returns for at least three years.

Valuable documents such as car titles, real estate deeds, stock certificates, bonds, insurance policies, contracts, leases, and warranties for major purchases should, of course, be kept indefinitely in a safe place—a fireproof metal lockbox or a safe deposit box at a bank. If you pay for something on an installment plan or with a loan, keep all payment records until the item is fully paid off.[13]

After your first job search and move, you should keep records of the cost of any future job searches (for example, résumé printing and travel to interviews) and moving expenses if you relocate for a new job. Some job hunting costs are deductible—if they are not for your first job, if you haven't been unemployed too long, and if you're not making a career change.[14] Even your first move could be deductible if the job you're moving to is located at least fifty miles from your former home.[15]

You may already have filed tax returns in the past, but once you start earning more money and having more expenses, you'll need to keep close track of your financial records. Both federal and state taxes (if you live in a state that has income tax) will be taken out of your paychecks. How much is deducted will depend on how many exemptions you claim on your withholding allowance certificate. Normally, a single person claims one exemption. You could claim more if you're paying real estate taxes and will claim a mortgage interest deduction on your tax return, if you will claim a lot of charitable contributions, or if you are responsible for children or other dependents. The more exemptions you claim, the less money will be taken out of your checks. If more money is taken out each month, you may be entitled to a refund after you file your returns by April 15. If you need more cash flow each month (for instance, to pay a mortgage loan), you can take more exemptions, but remember that you may have to pay some taxes when you file your return.

If your tax returns involve only very basic information (W-2 forms from your employer reporting taxes already withheld, savings account interest statement, stock dividend) you may choose to fill out and file your own tax returns. Tax laws change often, so follow the directions for your tax return form, and if you have questions call the 800 number listed in the instructions. The IRS also has a free publication, *Your Federal Income Tax,* which can be ordered by calling 1-800-829-3676. If you're into computers, there are many inexpensive software programs available to assist you with the preparation of your federal tax return. Many don't do individual state tax returns, however.

The 1040EZ tax form is most appropriate if you have a small salary from one job, or if you're a student. It's short and relatively easy to fill out, but you could wind up overlooking some deductions you're entitled to. The 1040 form comes in both long and short versions. The long one allows you to itemize deductions, which could result in a larger refund to you. There's a standard deduction ($3,900 for a single person in 1995; $6,550 for a married person filing a joint return for 1995), and if your itemized deductions are greater than the standard, it would be more advantageous for you to file the long form. If your itemized deductions total less than the standard deduction, you can file the short form unless you have self-employment income or gains or losses from the sale of stocks or bonds.[16] If you're owed a refund, file your papers as soon as you can to receive your money more quickly. If you owe taxes, wait to file your return and payment until closer to April 15, even if you prepare your return early. This will keep the money in your account as long as possible.

For basic tax returns you can use a commercial tax preparation service if you'd rather not do the return yourself or with the help of family or friends. If your financial situation or records are more complicated, you're better served by finding a professional accountant to prepare and file your return. Ask friends or relatives for recommendations, or perhaps someone at your new job can suggest an accountant in your new area. Just don't bring jumbled receipts in a shoebox on April 14!

Major Purchases

Chances are that you won't make too many large purchases immediately after graduation. Most apartments have a refrigerator and a stove, and many landlords provide access to a washer and a dryer in a laundry room. If you do buy a major appliance, or a smaller one such as a microwave oven, use resources such as *Consumer Reports* (back issues are often available at the library) to check on prices, frequency of repair records, and best buys. Comparison shop and get what you need rather than what a salesperson tries to convince you that you can't live without. A new appliance generally has a warranty period, often a year, covering defects. A dealer may try to sell you a service contract at extra cost. Look over the details of the service contract thoroughly. Consider how much more it really offers you above and beyond the manufacturer's warranty and whether it limits where you can have repairs done.

There is an implied warranty on all goods. That is, the law requires that any item sold be able to perform the function for which it was designed. For example, a toaster should toast and a radio should play. If the item doesn't do what it's supposed to do, you have the right to return it, and the dealer is obligated to replace or exchange it or to give you a credit or a refund. Stores should have their refund or exchange policy clearly posted; it is often found near the cashiers.[17]

Hold on to your receipt for anything you buy until you're sure it works satisfactorily. Keep a record of all your possessions, including the model and serial numbers, and send in all warranty or registration cards. Also record the purchase price and date for each item, and where you bought it. You'll need this information if you ever have to file an insurance claim (for example, theft or fire).[18] Keep the owner's manual on file. It will help if you have problems with the purchase, and it will also tell you where and how to seek service or repairs.

As a consumer, you have rights and resources to help you. Each state has a governmental service charged with protecting the rights of consumers. They're either listed in the phone book or can be found with the help of your library. Most areas also have a Better Business Bureau, which checks for honesty in advertising, keeps records about businesses in the area and complaints about them, and serves as an advocate for consumers in complaints about misrepresentation, poor service, and unresponsiveness to buyer complaints.[19] In addition, some cities have consumer complaint call-in segments on local news broadcasts. Representatives of the station pursue complaints that consumers have not been able to resolve through more direct channels. The publicity generated by this approach often persuades a reluctant merchant to do the right thing.

Buying a Car

Probably your largest purchase during the first few years after you graduate will be a car, if you decide to buy one. Before you begin shopping, think about what you're able to spend and what kind of car and options you want. Check with auto insurance companies first, since your insurance could cost you more if the car you buy is a high performance vehicle, is expensive to repair, or has a higher rate of theft. There may also be insurance discounts on cars that come with specific safety options such as automatic seat belts, air bags, or antilock brakes.[20]

Another resource is *Consumer Reports*. Their annual car roundup issue comes out in April. Find out about costs, options, frequency of repair records, safety features and tests, and gas mileage. If you're looking at used cars, the U.S. Department of Transportation Auto Safety Hotline (1-800-424-9393) provides information about cars that have been recalled and the reasons why.[21] Family members or friends who own different kinds of cars can share their experiences with you and help you narrow your focus.

While a used car is less expensive than a new one, it is also more risky. If you go to a dealer for a used car, look for the "Buyer's Guide" sticker on the car window. If you purchase a used car from a dealer, you should receive the original or a copy of that guide. Any changes in warranty coverage that you negotiate should be stated on the guide in writing. A used car may have a warranty that covers all or only some of the costs of service on that car. Read it carefully to determine the percentage of both labor and parts repair costs that the dealer will pay, the specific parts and systems (for example, the electrical system and the brakes) covered by the warranty, the duration of the warranty (such as sixty days or twenty-five hundred miles, whichever comes first) for each system, and whether any deductible applies. With a two-hundred-dollar deductible, you pay the first two hundred dollars for repairs.[22]

About half of the used cars sold by dealers and all of those sold privately are sold "as is." They do not come with warranties; if you have problems with one of those used cars, you will have to pay for all repairs yourself. Some states don't permit "as is" used car sales. Implied warranties will, however, generally exist unless the dealer tells you in writing that they don't. Implied warranties promise that the car will do what it's supposed to do—run, and serve the purpose the dealer says it will (for example, pull a trailer).[23]

If you're offered a service contract, consider what it will give you, for the price, that's not already covered by any warranty you receive. The value of a service contract is measured by whether the cost of repairs during the time you're covered is likely to be greater than the cost of the service contract.[24]

Before buying a used car, test drive it under a variety of conditions, especially those under which you will most often be using it. Also ask if the car has ever been in an accident and find out as much as you can about the car's history and maintenance record. If possible, talk to the last person who owned and drove the car. Have the car inspected by an experienced mechanic of your choice, not by one who works for the dealer or seller. Be prepared to try to negotiate the price or warranty coverage, or both, to get a deal that's more favorable to you.[25]

If you decide to purchase a new car rather than a used car, many of the same preparatory steps described for buying a used car also apply. In addition, some employers subscribe to an organization called United Buying Service. If your employer belongs, you can get information about car prices and perhaps be directed to some specific dealers. Know what you want and what you're prepared to spend. How many passengers will you usually carry? How much trunk space do you need? Will you be traveling long distances or commuting only a few miles every day?[26] Read up on road tests of new cars in *Consumer Reports, Motor Trend, Car and Driver,* or *Road and Track.*

Shop around at several different dealers to compare prices for the same models and options. Learn about specific car dealers by talking to people who have purchased cars from them. Most cars have logo labels or license plate frames on them, advertising the car dealer's name. When you see someone with a logo from a dealer you're considering, ask them about their experience there, their satisfaction with the car and the service, and so forth.[27] Most people are happy to share information, especially if they've had either a very positive or a very negative experience. You can also check out a dealer's service record by talking to car owners as they drop off or pick up their vehicles for servicing there. The Better Business Bureau and the Consumer Protection Agency can also provide information about dealers and any complaints that have been filed.[28]

When you visit dealers, ask specific questions and test drive any car you're interested in. How does it really feel to drive? To sit in? Can you be comfortable in this car for the purposes you want it to serve? The last time I was looking for a new car (after fifteen years of driving my first car), I test drove a Toyota Celica and was amazed at the power compared to my old Dodge Dart. I loved it. But getting in and out of the car with my long legs was another story. I knew I'd probably be in traction in a week if I had to get in and out of this car several times every day. I opted for another Toyota model. If a test drive doesn't give you all the information you need, you may be able to borrow a model you're seriously considering on a day when the dealership is closed. Or you could rent a similar model for a day or two to get a better feel for it over a period of time.[29]

> When you walk into a car dealership, you are entering Consumer Hell. There is no easy way to find out what the actual true price of any given car is. Oh, sure, there is a "sticker price," but only a very naive fungal creature just arrived from a distant galaxy would dream of paying this.
>
> —Dave Barry, "Where You Can Stick the Sticker Price"[30]

Plan to negotiate on price. Dealers may be willing to bargain on their profit margin between 10 and 20 percent, or the difference between the manufacturer's suggested retail price and the invoice price. You should be able to look up the wholesale dealer's price and suggested list price for any car and options in *Edmunds New Car Prices* or *Foreign Car Prices*. Consumers Union also puts out, for a small fee, price lists for each model. If you don't see the car you want with only the options you want, and you're not in a hurry, order your new car from the dealer. This may take longer, but you can avoid buying a car already on the lot with expensive options you may not want.[31] Some options such as a rear window defroster are necessities if you live in a cold, snowy climate. Others help the resale value of the car later on, such as air conditioning.

Only after getting the new car for the best negotiated price should you discuss the possibility of a trade-in, if you already have a car. Know how much your current car is worth so you can bargain effectively with the new car dealer. Check out the best price you could get from a used car dealer and compare that to what the dealer is offering you for the trade-in. Another option is for you to sell your old car on your own. This will take some time and energy, however.[32]

If you feel the offer for your trade-in is low, say so, and let them make another offer. When you agree on a price for the new car and the trade-in offer, the salesperson will fill out a buyer's order. Be sure to get everything in writing, including the delivery date and the specification that the sale price and trade-in value will be good until the new car is actually delivered.[33]

It's unlikely that you'll be able to pay for your car in full at the time of purchase. The larger the down payment you can afford and the more you can get for a trade-in, the smaller the loan you'll have to take out. Smaller loans mean less interest. Shop around for car loans. Check out several banks, starting with where you have an account or have done business before. If you belong to a credit union, get a quote from them, and compare all these to the financing rate the dealer offers you. Get each potential lender's offer in writing, including how long they'll hold it open. The offer should include the principal amount of the loan, the amount of each monthly payment, and the number of payments. Multiply the amount of each monthly payment by the number of monthly payments and subtract the total from the principal amount of the loan to see what the finance charges are. Don't faint![34]

If a service contract is suggested, compare it with what you're already getting under the manufacturer's warranty. Don't pay again for coverage you already have.[35] Information about automobile insurance is covered later in this chapter.

One more important point—buying the car is just the beginning. Maintaining the car and keeping it in good shape is an ongoing job. Service your car as suggested in the owner's manual. Preventive maintenance is cheaper than emergency repairs. Get written estimates for any work to be done. Find a mechanic you trust to oversee your car maintenance on a regular basis, someone who won't tell you that you need something done if it doesn't need to be done, someone you can believe when she or he says something is necessary. Ask people in the area whom they use and trust, and trust your own instincts once you meet and deal with the mechanic. Become knowledgeable yourself about car maintenance and repair. Continuing education or adult education courses on car maintenance and repair can teach you how to do basic work such as changing the oil yourself and give you the confidence to ask the right questions and avoid being taken advantage of when others do work for you. You may decide to belong to an auto club, such as AAA, which provides the security of nationwide assistance and help when, for example, you get a flat tire or need to be towed.[36]

If you need transportation but prefer not to go the car buying route, an alternative is to lease a car. When you lease a car you pay a monthly fee for a specified period of time and maximum mileage.[37] Comparison shop for leasing a car as you would for buying one. Get the best deal you can. Try to lease without having to make a down payment, or at least look for a low down payment. Find out who is responsible for upkeep and repairs and how much a full maintenance contract would add to your monthly fee.[38] An advantage of leasing is that it's simple and convenient and you don't have to take out a car loan and pay interest on that loan. In addition, after your leasing contract is up, you can lease a newer model.

While leasing reduces your up-front and monthly payments, it can wind up costing more in the long run. When you finish a leasing contract, you have nothing to show for it and have to start all over with a new lease and monthly payments. When you buy a car, you pay it off within three to five years and keep the ownership of that car and its residual value for years after that, with only the cost of upkeep and repairs.[39]

Another auto option is to rent a car when you need one. This alternative is good if you drive little and use public transportation much of the time. City dwellers for the most part will want to rent what they need when they need it: a small car for a day trip to the beach, a van to help move furniture, and so forth. City renters save on garage, maintenance, and insurance costs.[40]

Credit Cards

> It's almost as bad to have no credit rating at all as it is to have a poor one.   —M.E.

Credit cards have been described both as a godsend and as the devil in plastic coating. The challenge is to use credit wisely in order to build a good credit history without incurring a debt that you have to spend perhaps the next ten years of your life trying to pay off. A general rule is that the total of all your credit card and loan payments each month (for example, car loan and student loan) should be *less* than 20 percent of your monthly take-home pay.[41] If your credit charges take you above 20 percent, you should cut back on your credit card use.

Credit cards can be dangerous because they're so easy to use. Then the bills come in. The key to developing a good credit history is to charge only the amount you can afford to pay back on time. Make every effort to pay the bills in full each month.

> With minimum payments these days hovering around 2 percent, consumers who only cover that minimum payment are barely putting a dent in the principal each month. For example, if you

> owe $5,000 and pay 2.5 percent of that each month, it'll take
> you a little more than 24 years to pay it off. And with an annual
> percentage rate of 17 percent, you'll have paid more than $6,000
> in interest—more than your initial principal.
>
> —Ruth Susswein, Bankcard Holders of America[42]

Keep track of your charges. You could use a notebook or put all the receipts in one place whenever you charge anything. Know how much you've got charged at any one time. Use this information when you review your monthly statement to catch any mistakes.

If you qualify for general credit cards such as VISA, MasterCard, or Discover, get only one of them. The more cards you have, the easier it is to lose track of charges and run up bills beyond the 20 percent rule. Most department stores and gas stations now accept the major general credit cards, so it's not necessary to accumulate a large number of specialized cards. Aim toward having "the fewest number of cards to serve the greatest number of needs at the lowest possible cost."[43]

Decide which credit card is best for you by exploring the terms and features each offers and what best meets your needs. Fees and charges on cards will vary depending on the issuing bank. Shop around. You're also not limited to banks within your immediate geographic area.[44] The Truth in Lending Act requires that you be provided with the information you need to make wise choices when you apply for credit. The fine print on your credit card application and on the reverse side of your monthly statement provides this information.[45]

First, what is the annual percentage rate (APR) or the cost of interest on your outstanding credit balance on a yearly basis? This isn't a big issue if you always pay your bill in full each month. American Express is an example of a charge card that requires you to do this. Second, what is the annual fee for the card? Third, is there a grace period that allows you to pay the balance without any finance charge before a "due date" noted on the monthly statement? If there's a grace period, the credit card company must mail your bill at least fourteen days before your payment is due. Without a grace period, a finance charge will be imposed from the date you charge something or the date the charge is posted to your account. The latter is more desirable. Fourth, are there any other charges or fees (for cash advances, late payments, going over your credit limit, and so forth)? Fifth, are there other services or features that are important to you, such as automatic teller capability, wide acceptance of the card, reduced-rate travel insurance and car rentals, or accumulation of frequent flyer miles for every dollar charged? [46]

If you cannot qualify for a major credit card right away, you can slowly build up to it. Open a checking or savings account, or both, at a local bank. Canceled checks can be used as evidence that you pay bills regularly. If you've lived in the same area for at least a year and have a steady income, apply for credit with a local business like a department store. Charge amounts that you can pay off promptly, and do so. You can also borrow a small amount from your bank and pay it off promptly. Some banks will issue you a bank credit card with a credit limit no greater than the amount you have on deposit. Use that credit card responsibly. It will help build your credit history and eventually expand your line of credit. If you don't qualify for a card on the basis of your own credit standing, a relative might be able to cosign your application. Failure to pay your credit card bills on time under this condition, however, will affect not only your credit rating but also that of your cosigner.

If you apply for credit in hopes of establishing your history, ask whether your creditor reports credit history information to the credit bureaus that serve your area. Try to get credit that will be reported this way. Three large credit bureaus keep track of credit records. If you have had credit before under another name, ask the credit bureau to include it. If you share an account with a partner, ask to have the account recorded in both of your names so it will contribute to your credit history. On the other hand, if you share an account with someone who is irresponsible, that shared credit history can hurt you in the future.

If you're rejected for credit, you have a right to find out why. If a creditor rejects your application because of negative information in your credit bureau report, she or he must tell you which bureau was involved; you can then request your credit file from them. You also have a right to contest the accuracy of any information. Credit bureaus are legally required to report bankruptcies for ten years and other negative information for seven years.[47]

Don't mess up on your loans and credit cards. Pay them at least something every month. If you can't, it will haunt you for the rest of your life.   —F.J.

Good faith efforts to work out payment plans with creditors are far better than trying to avoid the situation. If you dig yourself into a hole, try contacting a consumer credit counseling office. This nonprofit organization will work with you to develop a plan to repay your creditors. They'll also help you set up a more constructive approach for the future.[48]

Doonesbury

BY GARRY TRUDE,

Doonesbury, copyright © 1994 by G. B. Trudeau. Reprinted with permission of Universal Press Syndicate. All rights reserved.

Your credit history will include information about your repayment of loans. This includes any student loans you have taken out. Recent data indicates that 12.5 million U.S. workers are slowly paying off almost $2 billion in college loans. One survey estimated that an undergraduate degree carries with it an average debt of almost eight thousand dollars.[49]

Be sure you understand exactly what you're obligated to do to pay off your student loans. Your college financial aid office will have exit interviews to explain the procedures, and representatives of the lending institutions will answer questions. It's important that you pay off your loans according to schedule. There is a six- to nine-month grace period before you have to begin paying. Student loans carry a relatively low interest rate, so it's to your advantage to pay them off according to the schedule and to use your cash flow to pay for more immediate expenses that carry a higher interest rate than your loan does.[50]

If you're in a low-paying job and can't keep up with your loan payments, contact the lender. You may be able to arrange for lower monthly payments for a while. Some postgraduate plans, like graduate or professional school, can permit you to defer payment on your loans (but may also lead to additional loans). You'll need to complete and return to the lender a deferral form each semester you're enrolled in graduate school. Even if you'll be eligible for a deferment in a year or two, you can demonstrate good faith by starting to repay your loan.

Individual state higher education agencies may have programs that allow you to work in some specific jobs (for example, teaching in low-income areas or teaching in subject areas where there's a high demand) and get a reduction in your loan. Check with the agency in the state of your legal residence.

Banking

Bank accounts can help you save and keep track of your money. Understand the different options in order to select the

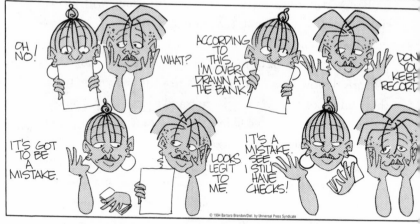

Where I'm Coming From, copyright © 1994 by Barbara Brandon. Distributed by Universal Press Syndicate. Reprinted with permission. All rights reserved.

one that best meets your needs and financial situation. There are four basic types of accounts to consider:

Checking
Savings
Money market
Time deposits or certificates of deposit (CDs)[51]

A checking account gives you quick and convenient access to your money. You may also be able to use an automated teller machine (ATM) to deposit, withdraw, or transfer funds twenty-four hours a day. Some checking accounts pay interest; others don't. Fees will vary and can include monthly maintenance fees (either routinely or only if you fall below a stated balance) or charges for checks or ATM transactions.

Generally, interest-bearing checking accounts have higher fees and require large minimum balances, so be wary of committing to an account that involves paying more in fees than you earn in interest.[52]

One fee option you can elect for a checking account provides you with overdraft protection. This gives you a line of credit that covers any overdrafts, up to the amount of your credit line, and reduces the risk of your bouncing a check, which often carries a large fine. This protection will appeal to some of you; others will decide that it would make you less careful than you should be. In any event, balance your checkbook as soon as your monthly statement arrives. The back of each statement explains how to do this.

Many banks offer very basic accounts, with a limited set of services, at low cost to you. These are usually checking accounts but with a limit on the number of checks you can write and the number of deposits and withdrawals you can make. Compare basic and regular checking accounts at different banks for the lowest fees, the lowest minimum balance you're required to keep, and the fewest restrictions on use.[53]

Savings accounts earn you interest at an annual percentage rate stated by the banking institution. You can make withdrawals or transfers from a savings account, but the number of these transactions may be limited. A fee will be assessed if you go over that number. You may also be required to maintain a minimum balance to avoid fees.[54]

Money market accounts are interest-bearing accounts that allow you to write checks on them. These accounts generally pay a higher rate of interest than regular savings accounts, but a higher minimum deposit is required to establish them.

There may be a limit on the number of transfers or checks you can write on a money market account each month, or there may be a minimum amount for which a check can be written.[55]

Time deposits or certificates of deposit (CDs) usually offer a guaranteed rate of interest for a specified term that can range from several days to several years. Once you choose a term, you cannot withdraw the money until the term ends or the deposit matures. In exchange for leaving your funds in this account for the specified period of time, you receive a higher rate of interest than for a savings or a money market account. Generally, the longer term you select, the higher the annual percentage yield of interest. There is a hefty penalty fee for early withdrawal. CDs also often renew automatically unless you let the bank know that you want to take your money out at maturity.[56]

In deciding what type of account or accounts to open, consider how much access to your money you will need. If you expect to have to pay bills monthly, you're better off with a checking account, perhaps combined with a savings account that will earn you some interest. Keep any excess funds in your interest-earning savings account rather than just sitting in your checking account. You can always shift over what you need. If you write only one or two checks a month, you could earn a higher rate of interest by putting your money in a money market deposit account. If you want to build up savings and will not need money soon, a certificate of deposit can earn you the most interest.[57]

Credit unions are nonprofit cooperatives made up of individuals with some kind of bond—a union, a particular company, a professional organization, and so forth. Because credit unions are nonprofit, they are exempt from federal taxes and don't have the same restrictions as banks. Credit unions can thus offer higher interest rates, lower required minimum deposits, fewer service charges, and reasonably priced loans.[58] If your employer belongs to a credit union, check out its services in comparison with those at the banks you're considering.

Banks and credit unions are legally required to disclose full information about their services and fees. Read the fine print, and consult with an officer of the bank or credit union to ask all the questions you need to in order to make the best decision. One intangible factor to consider in choosing a bank or credit union is how you're treated by the people who work there. No matter how small your account, you should be treated with respect and in a friendly and patient manner. Compare the features of different banks and credit unions available to you. Is there a minimum balance required to open an account? What is the annual percentage yield or amount of interest you'll earn on a deposit? Is there a minimum balance required before you can start earning interest? Is there a particular balance above which you will earn an even higher interest rate? Do you begin earning interest on the day you deposit a check or later, when the bank or credit union receives credit for it? Is the interest compounded, that is, does the bank or credit union pay interest on the interest you've already earned? If you close your account before the end of a quarter, do you lose all interest for that quarter? What fees are assessed, and for what reasons? Are fees waived if you keep a minimum balance in your account? Are minimum balances considered daily or as the average during a statement cycle? If the average balance is used, you won't be charged a fee if you fall below the minimum balance for a week as long as your average balance for the month is above that minimum. Can you get checking account fees waived by maintaining a minimum balance in a savings account at the same bank or credit union? [59]

There are other features that might be important to you. For example, can you get ATM card privileges, and are there any fees for those privileges? Will you be eligible for a bank credit card? Can you make telephone transfers, and are there any fees involved?

Some of you will prefer to make choices that give you the easiest possible access to your money. Others will find more safety in not being able to, for example, use an ATM twenty-four hours a day or cash an unlimited number of checks. You may choose to pass up some features in order to help yourself manage your finances most efficiently.

Your employer may offer a direct deposit option—whereby your regular paycheck is automatically sent to your bank or credit union and deposited into your account. This has several advantages. Sometimes it's easier to save if the cash doesn't actually pass through your hands first. Direct deposit also saves time and hassle on your part. You don't have to arrange your life to get to the bank or credit union to deposit the check. Lines can be long and frustrating. If paying your monthly bills is dependent on your check deposit, a delay in getting that deposit made can threaten your ability to pay those bills on time. Some banks or credit unions can also direct deposit a predetermined amount of each check into savings, and automatically take care of some of your monthly loan payments.

If you're moving a distance, closing an account in one city, and planning to open a new one in the place you're headed, talk to your old bank or credit union about the process for closing out your accounts there. Don't leave any outstanding checks uncovered, or they'll bounce. Don't carry large sums of cash with you. This may be a good time to use a credit card or get traveler's checks to take care of initial expenses and open your new account. They're like instant cash. A cashier's check from your old bank can also be used to open your new account. With a cashier's check, you should be able to write checks on your new balance within a few days after you make your opening deposit.

Employment Benefits

When you discuss your benefits options during a job negotiation, you may feel like a contestant on *Let's Make a Deal*. Which medical plan do you choose? Do you want additional life insurance? How much? How many tax exemptions do you declare? Do you go for more cash in your take-home pay or opt for specific benefits? Do you want what's behind the door or curtain number two?! If your employer offers you the option of receiving pay checks every two weeks or every month, consider the due dates of your regular bills and when you need to have the funds available. It can be risky to cut the turn-around time too closely, so consider more frequent paychecks if you're given that option.

Other types of benefits can seem confusing and overwhelming, particularly in the midst of decisions you're making about whether to accept the job itself. Many people believe that the benefits package you're offered is as important as your starting salary and needs to be given as much, if not more, attention. For every one hundred dollars employees receive in direct salary, it costs employers an additional forty dollars to cover fringe benefits—retirement, health insurance, paid vacations, life insurance, and so forth.[60] The personnel or human resources development office should provide information for all employees about benefits. Many also publish employee handbooks or manuals and distribute or post information. There are a number of key benefits to consider as you make job decisions, and you'll have additional decisions to make about each of these benefits.

Health or medical insurance is an important consideration. (This issue is covered in detail in chapter 6 on health care.) Bear in mind, however, that most employers will periodically (annually) offer an open enrollment period during which you can change from one health insurance plan to another without penalty. These periods follow information meetings to help you assess your needs and the options available to you.

The law requires that your employer provide worker's compensation, unemployment insurance, and social security benefits. A percentage of your salary is taken out for social security for your eventual retirement. This amount is also matched by your employer.

Pension plans or retirement programs are offered by many employers to supplement social security coverage. Participate as soon as you are eligible (there may be a year or more

QUALITY TIME   Gail Machlis

waiting period or a minimum age after which you can join). Money put into retirement plans is not taxed until you retire, and often employers will match the employee contribution.

If that's the case, for every dollar you invest in your retirement fund, your employer could be giving a matching dollar. Money invested in retirement now will be of great benefit to you later, even though it's hard to look so far into the future.

The 401(k) program is a current retirement program being offered in some companies to defer a portion of your salary and matching employer funds toward your retirement and exclude it from federal taxes. You'll pay no taxes on that money until you retire, at which point you're likely to be in a lower tax bracket. The disadvantage of a 401(k) is that you won't have access to that money for decades, until you retire. If you withdraw money before that, you'll pay income taxes on what you withdraw plus a penalty fee.[61] If your employer offers a 401(k) program, *take advantage of it.*

In most cases you have a choice where you want your 401(k) contributions invested—for example, in fixed income funds, money market funds, conservative equity funds, growth equity funds. You can diversify your investments among the different options offered. Consider earmarking some of your monthly contribution into growth oriented investments. While the risk is greater in the short term, the potential for rewards is also greater. As a younger person, you have time to change your investment strategy if this investment doesn't perform as well as you had hoped.[62]

Other employment benefits to look for include life insurance and disability insurance. Your employer may provide a certain amount of coverage, giving you the option to purchase additional amounts. Educational assistance plans for you and your family, help with child care expenses, dental plans, and some forms of profit sharing may also be available. If you're planning to start a family in the near future, your employer's policy on paid vacations, sick days, and maternity leave will be of interest to you.

Investments

Individual retirement accounts (IRAs) are available through banks and also through private investment counselors. IRAs are put into a variety of investments, and the moneys grow with taxes deferred. This means that you pay no taxes on that money until it's withdrawn. The funds cannot be taken out without penalty (except for one or two special circumstances, such as if you become totally disabled) before you reach the age of fifty-nine and a half, and they must begin to be taken out by the time you're seventy and a half. IRAs are good tax savings investments.

Outside of stocks and bonds that may be part of an IRA, you probably won't be in a financial position to be able to invest in stocks or bonds for a while. If and when you have the funds to consider making some investments, consult with a financial planner or an investment firm to discuss your options. Unless you have enough knowledge to research and understand the market yourself, look for a full service broker. Work with someone you trust and whose approach to investing your money is responsive to your priorities and concerns.

Do whatever you can do, from the start of your work career, to save, invest, or otherwise regularly direct money, especially pretax dollars, into savings, retirement, IRA, and other investments. In your early twenties it can be hard to think about your life at sixty-five. The earlier you start saving, however, the more interest your money will accumulate, and the better you will be providing for yourself and your family way down the road.

Insurance

See chapter 4 for information about renter's or tenant's insurance. Chapter 6 includes a discussion of health insurance, since decisions about health insurance and health care providers are closely tied together. There are several other insurance issues to consider.

Shop around for both an insurance company and an agent. Compare policies, coverage, and costs. Ask friends, check the yellow pages, or call the state insurance department for referrals. *Consumer Reports* examines and rates insurance companies based on customer satisfaction. *Best Insurance Reports* and *Standard and Poor's* (available in the library) also rate insurance companies. Quotesmith (1-800-556-9393) is a free insurance price comparison service. This company tracks rates, coverage, and financial stability ratings of leading insurance companies in a continually updated information database. They will, upon request, develop a comprehensive report in response to your needs and can assist you in comparing prices by computer.[63]

Look for financial comparisons and stability. Get prices from several agents who deal exclusively with one company. Prices can vary between different companies and even with different agents from the same insurance company. See what the best deal is you can get from each, and then settle on the best of the best. Some companies will also give you a discount if you get more than one type of insurance policy (for example, auto and renter's) from them.

You'll find some independent agents or insurance brokers who deal with a number of different companies. On one hand, this approach can give you a variety of options in one location with an agent who will do the shopping around for you to find the best deal. On the other hand, you don't really know whether this agent is quoting you prices and coverage that best meet your needs, or whether the motive is to best meet *his* or *her* needs and bring her or him the highest commissions.

> Because I live in Los Angeles, where car insurance is both manda-
> tory and unobtainable, I was involved in an accident with people
> who had no insurance. Luckily, I'm insured for that. But in
> checking the fine print on my policy, not for collision. Not for
> collision? What am I insured for . . . near misses?
>
> —Rita Rudner, "Rethinking Chapter 31"[64]

If you have a car, you are legally required to carry certain amounts of automobile insurance. Collision, liability (bodily injury and property damage), comprehensive (fire and theft), and uninsured and underinsured motorist coverages are available. Check the requirements in your state. Your automobile insurance should cover you when driving any vehicle, including borrowed or rental cars.[65] You can lower your costs by increasing your deductibles (the amount you need to pay yourself before the insurance company will pay) on collision and comprehensive categories. Your rates will also be influenced by the kind of car you drive, how you use it (for pleasure, for commuting), your past driving record, your age, your gender, your marital status, the number of children you have, where you live and keep the car, and whether you're the principal driver. Insurance agents look for indications of your stability and responsibility.

If you've been covered under your parents' policy, you may get your best deal as a spin-off by that company onto your own policy. Discounts may also be available if you drive fewer than a specific number of miles in a year, live in a rural community, have certain safety features on your car, get good grades in school, or have a good driving record.[66]

In looking for car insurance, one alternative to dealing with an agent is to work with a direct marketing company with no agents or commissions. These companies advertise that they can pass along these savings to their customers. Word of mouth is the best way to find out about direct marketing companies.

Regardless of where you insure your car, you'll need the following information for your policy application.

Driver's license number

Social security number

Number of years at your present address

Vehicle information—make, type, year, serial number (your registration and title will have this information)

Information about your education, how long you've been licensed, how long you've been driving

A three-year history of your driving record, including

any tickets or accidents (date, amount of damage, who was at fault)

You'll need proof of insurance coverage when you register your car. The insurance company will also run a check on all the information you provide and review all your past claims and driving history.

If you are responsible for any dependents (a partner, children, a parent, for instance), consider purchasing two other types of insurance if your employment benefits don't provide them. Disability insurance compensates for income you're likely to lose if you're incapacitated or hospitalized for an extended amount of time—beyond the paid sick days you're entitled to. If your income is your sole source of support or if it supports any dependents, consider obtaining disability insurance.

If you have no dependents, the decision to buy life insurance may be less immediately crucial. Be aware, though, that you may not always be as easily and cheaply insurable as you are when you're younger and healthier. There are two types of life insurance. Term life insurance policies are issued for a certain amount of coverage for a specific number of years. If you die, the policy will pay your beneficiaries the face value of the policy. Term policy coverage ends when it expires, usually after a year, but it can be renewed until you reach the age of sixty-five. Premiums increase each year as you grow older but are still less expensive than those for whole life insurance policies.[67]

Whole life insurance policies are one type of cash value

insurance. They serve two purposes by having a cash value beyond their face value. They combine insurance protection in case of death with a tax deferred savings plan. The whole life policy builds a cash value, and you can borrow against it if you ever have to.[68] For a single person just out of college and not covered by life insurance as a job benefit, term policies offer the most coverage at the lowest cost. If you go this route, ask if your insurance company will let you convert your term policy into whole life later on.[69]

New college graduates rarely think about needing a will. While it's advisable for everyone to have a will, it's especially important if you're married, about to get married, have a partner you want to provide for, have children, or own significant assets. A will assures that your property is distributed according to your wishes, that the person of your choice is the executor of your financial affairs, managing what you leave behind, and that the person you designate becomes the guardian of your dependent children.[70] Consult with a lawyer to draw up a will. There are many books or kits available on how to write your own will. You can save some time (and lawyers charge by the hour!) by reviewing some of these resources first and preparing for the questions a lawyer will ask.

Doctor, Doctor, Give Me the News: Health Care

Before I left for college as a freshman, my grandmother took it upon herself to help me stock up on things she thought I would need. In restaurants she would take a few extra packets of sugar, press them into my hand, and whisper, "So you'll have some for your tea." She had always given me tea, with sugar, when I was sick. Even though I figured I could always get sugar, even in the wilds of upstate New York, I took the packets. In my grandmother's eyes, they were something tangible to help me take care of myself. Maybe I saw them that way too.

Starting Early

Stock up on the *in*tangibles while you're still at college— healthy habits and routines. This can create a lifestyle so ingrained in your way of being that it will carry over once you graduate. Habits, whether good ones or bad ones, tend to continue, so make yours good ones.

Develop healthy eating habits throughout your college years. Limit fast food and fat intake, and include lots of fruits and vegetables. Contrary to popular belief, you can even acquire good eating habits in the college dining hall. Some food services have staff nutritionists, and others provide nutritional information about each meal.

Start developing a routine exercise program early. Your choice of physical education classes can introduce you to a wide range of activities, including those that you can continue throughout your life. The physical education facilities on campus (for example, the pool, the weight room) provide free opportunities for discovering new ways to exercise. Do aerobics with friends. Jog. Lift weights. Go dancing. Take a walk before breakfast or after dinner. Discover a routine that works for you and keep it up. Graduate school or the working world can be stressful places, especially when you're making the transition and changing your lifestyle. An enduring exercise routine may need to be adapted to a new schedule or situation, but if it's strong enough, it can withstand the other changes in your life.

Learn to handle stress early, and recognize your body's signals that tell you stress is getting in your way. Many schools offer wellness programs or classes. Take advantage of them. Learn early how to control and manage your own stress levels.

Be smart about your sexual and drinking choices and behaviors. If you're in good health, have a basic physical every four or five years (including blood work, blood pressure, cholesterol check, and so forth). If you have any kind of ongoing health condition that needs to be watched, follow the advice of your health care provider. If you're a woman, have a PAP smear done annually.

Your Health History and Records

When was your last tetanus shot? What year did you have your tonsils out? Tough questions for you to answer? When you apply for insurance or seek new health care providers after you graduate, you'll be asked to provide this kind of detail about your medical history. Collect this information early. Keep thorough medical records and an accurate medical history for yourself.

Your childhood doctor or health care provider should be able to give you a copy of your history, including dates of immunizations and vaccinations, when you had various childhood diseases, and the dates of any surgeries or accidents. If you were ever treated elsewhere (maybe at a hospital when you had appendicitis in summer camp), include that information. Some of these events may come back to you by talking with your family members. Also, document any history of diseases in your family. For example, does breast cancer run in your family? Did any of your relatives have heart problems? Family history can help a doctor to assess your risk factors for some diseases. It's a lot easier to have all this information at your fingertips in a notebook than to sit in a doctor's office after you've graduated, counting back on your fingers to figure out just when you had the measles.

Senior Year

If you haven't pulled together your medical history by this time, do it now. The easiest way at this point would be to request, in writing, that the college health service give you a copy of your file at the end of the year or send it to your new health care provider. This would include the medical form your health care provider from home completed before you entered college, any baseline imaging records such as an EKG or a mammogram, and any examination and treatment notes generated during your college years. You have a right to your medical files and records. Take all this material with you when you relocate and establish yourself with a new health care provider.

When you're getting ready to graduate, take advantage of any lower-cost procedures or medications available on campus—routine physicals, PAP smear, birth control pills. Costs will generally be greater on the outside, so do what you can before you leave. Also take advantage of any educational programs offered to teach students about preventive health care.

Finally, find out what your health insurance situation will be once you graduate. If you have college health insurance, does your policy terminate when you graduate? On the last day of the month when you graduate? Some college health plans will cover graduates through late August.

Making the Transition

> Don't let the medical world—from physicians to insurance companies—intimidate you.   —W.M., nurse practitioner

Health Insurance

If you're young and relatively healthy, health insurance may feel like a less pressing expense when you're juggling a lot of financial obligations as a new graduate. It's actually very pressing. Health insurance coverage is a major benefit to consider when job hunting. If you don't have a job with health benefits lined up before your current coverage runs out, consider one of several alternatives.

Graduates under the age of twenty-three who are listed as dependents have a legal option to "roll over" their college insurance into their parents' plan until they turn twenty-three.[1] If you've been carried on your parents' plan throughout college, find out how long and under what conditions you can stay on that plan until you get your own coverage, either an individual policy or one obtained through a group plan where you work. Under a federal law called COBRA, you can continue coverage under your parents' plan, but you would need to pay the full cost of the premium plus a small fee to the employer.[2]

Another option is a temporary short-term individual insurance plan that provides coverage for anywhere from one month to six months. Temporary policies won't cover preexisting conditions, however, and you cannot be covered if you're pregnant. These plans are designed for those between jobs, recent college graduates, and those waiting to be covered under a group policy in a new job. If you'll be attending graduate or professional school full time, your university may offer student insurance to those enrolled in graduate programs. Check out that possibility.

Temporary short-term policy rates are lower than the third option, a permanent individual policy for a year or more. If you're working at a part-time job or for an employer who does not offer health insurance benefits, or if you have completed the maximum number of months you can be covered on a temporary short-term plan, consider individual health insurance. Your premium rate will be the amount you pay the insurance company each billing period (for example, monthly or quarterly) to receive your health insurance coverage. Your rates will be affected by your age, the area of the country in which you live, whether or not you smoke, and how high a deductible you're willing to pay.[3] The deductible is the amount you have to pay for medical bills before you can start to collect from the insurance company. Your premium payments for your policy will be lower if you have a higher deductible. For example, the premiums on a $500 deductible policy are lower than those for one with a $200 deductible. With the former, however, you have to pay $500 in medical bills before the insurance company will pay, while with the latter the company will begin paying after you've covered $200 in bills. It's generally desirable to take as large a deductible as you can afford.[4]

For example, I carried an individual health insurance policy for four years when I was not receiving benefits. I looked over the insurance information and saw that if I took a $200 deductible, I would pay $135 a month—$1,620 a year—in premiums. If I took a $500 deductible, I would pay $107 a month—$1,284 a year. It would cost me $336 more a year to get the lower deductible. I considered my pattern of yearly medical costs and realized that in order to benefit from the lower deductible I would have to incur $536 of medical costs during the year before I would receive any reimbursement. Based on my past medical expenses, which consistently fell below $536, I decided to go for the higher deductible and the lower premium. I knew that if I had to, I could cover the $500 deductible if I had unexpectedly high medical costs in one particular year. It felt like a reasonable risk to take, and I saved $336 a year.

If your insurance covers a percentage of your costs after you reach a deductible level, you can also lower your monthly premiums by agreeing to a higher copayment. For most policies, a 20 percent copayment is desirable. This means that after your deductible is reached, the insurance company pays 80 percent of the cost and you pay 20 percent.[5]

If you get married right after graduation, and your partner has health insurance benefits at his or her job, or you both have these benefits, check out all your coverage possibilities. It may be advantageous to both be covered under one partner's plan. If so, you may need to make some payments to expand that partner's individual coverage under the group plan to include the spouse or other family members. Take into account the security of the job under which you'd both be covered.

Generally, health insurance tends to help with more major problems (surgery, an accident, a hospital stay) rather than with the more routine services. Some policies, however, have an eye toward prevention, and they will offer preventive care benefits such as gynecological exams and mammograms. The cost to the patient may be only a small copayment charge unless additional treatment is needed.

State insurance departments provide useful information about the strength and stability of insurance companies you may be considering. They also have information about consumer complaints. *Consumer Reports, Best Insurance Reports,* and *Standard and Poor's* all rate insurance companies. Quotesmith (1-800-556-9393) is a free insurance comparison service that tracks rates, coverage, and financial stability ratings of leading insurance companies in a continually updated information database. They will, upon request, develop a comprehensive report in response to your needs and can assist you in comparing prices by computer.[6]

As you weigh health insurance plans, whether they're individual plans bought on your own or options offered by your employer, consider what services are covered and to what degree (for example, in full, 80 percent after the deductible is paid, or with a copayment of ten dollars for any office visit). What is your deductible, or the amount you're responsible for paying yourself before the insurance will pay? Are prescription drugs covered under the plan? Are preexisting conditions (for example, asthma or diabetes) fully covered? Partially covered? Are routine preventive benefits included even if they don't reach the deductible? Look for a policy that best covers what you need, rather than paying for coverage you don't need. Look also at the fine print for a guaranteed renewal clause. With this clause in your policy, the company can't drop you just because your health becomes worse.[7] A good policy should cover all or most of the following:[8]

Inpatient hospital services
Surgical services
Ambulance
Doctors' visits (office and hospital)
Newborn services
Children's medical expenses (to age nineteen or twenty-
   three if full-time students)
Maternity care
Preventive care and checkups
Prescription medication
Lab tests and X rays
Home health care
Physical therapy
Psychiatric and mental health services
Drug and alcohol abuse treatment
Hospice care

Another provision to consider, for a higher premium payment, is the stop loss provision. This places a limit on the amount of medical expenses you have to pay each year and protects you from being financially wiped out by a major illness or accident. If you incur a very large medical expense without the stop loss provision, you will have to pay your full deductible and your copayment for all bills after that deductible is reached. Twenty percent (if that's your copayment) of one hundred thousand dollars, for example, would be twenty thousand dollars on top of your deductible. With the stop loss provision, however, once your contribution reaches a prearranged amount, any medical expenses above and beyond that limit for the rest of the year will be paid 100 percent by the insurance company.[9]

Many employers offer an open enrollment period annually, during which you can change your health care plan without incurring any fee or penalty. This is especially important if you become dissatisfied with your current plan or services or if your situation changes, for example if you want to cover your partner or if you consider having a child.

Know how to file a claim. Some medical offices will automatically do the paperwork for you, once they've made a copy of your insurance card information. They may accept your insurance and then bill you only for anything the company doesn't pay them for. Other medical offices will ask you for some or all of the payment up front, at the time you're seen. They will then reimburse you once they receive payment from your insurance company. Some offices will have you pay up front, and you will be responsible for filing your insurance claim form on your own. The company will either credit your claim to your deductible total or reimburse you if your deductible has been reached. Keep all your original medical receipts, and send copies when you have to document your claim. Be sure to submit all claims as soon as possible so your insurance company will know when you've reached your deductible and their payments should start.[10]

If you feel you have a claim rejected unfairly, you can appeal to the insurance company. Explain the provisions in your policy that you feel justify your claim, and ask for a written explanation of why it was denied.[11] The state insurance commissioner acts as a watchdog over the insurance industry. If you're unable to resolve a disputed claim with the company, contact the commissioner's office.[12]

Health Care Providers

Nowadays, health insurance and health care providers are becoming increasingly interrelated. If you're receiving a health plan as an employee benefit, your employer will choose its insurance carrier or carriers (some companies will give you a choice), and each carrier defines the network of doctors or other providers they cover. Private indemnity insurance that gives you a totally free choice of doctors and hospitals is generally the most expensive. Preferred provider networks offer you a list of doctors and health care providers, and hospitals, who are covered under their insurance plan. These doctors could be in private practice, working as part of a group, or operating from an office in a hospital or medical center. Some doctors are members of more than one network. You would choose a primary care physician from this network, although some plans let you see someone outside the network if you're willing to pay a fee for stepping outside.

There are number of questions you should ask. Which health care providers are in each network that you are considering? This may be important if you're already seeing a particular doctor you really like or if a particular doctor has been recommended to you. How much choice will you have about which health care providers you see? What costs or penalties are there if you step out of the network to see someone else (Do you need your primary care physician's approval? Do you have to pay the full charge? Does the expense count toward your deductible?)?

Health Maintenance Organizations (HMOs) tend to be less expensive than preferred provider networks, but they also offer fewer options and choices. HMOs provide health services for a fixed prepaid premium. There are usually no deductibles, only small copayments for visits, and you don't have to fill out insurance claim forms. Out-of-pocket expenses are minimal.[13] If you belong to an HMO, you will have a primary care physician who will oversee your health care and refer you, if needed, to specialists. Depending on the particular HMO, you may or may not be able to choose your primary care physician or specialist. Some HMOs that are clinic-type organizations require you to see whichever doctor is on duty when you have an appointment. If your HMO allows some choice of physicians, selecting someone with more investment in the success of the organization (for example, a doctor who is on the board of directors of the HMO) may be a good approach. This doesn't guarantee anything, but someone who has a greater commitment to the smooth running and success of the organization may be especially responsive to patients. If you're dissatisfied with your care at an HMO, these facilities often have patient advocates or an ombudsperson. State attorney general's offices have health advocacy units to handle complaints.

There are a variety of other sources of health care to consider. A hospital emergency room *shouldn't* be a substitute for routine medical care. You'll encounter a long wait, medical personnel who know little about your overall health, and expensive fees, and your insurance company may not cover this inappropriate use of an emergency room.

Storefront-type walk-in immediate care centers are located in some areas of the country. These facilities treat individuals on a walk-in basis, first come, first served. These clinics handle less severe conditions, and while they're less expensive than an emergency room, they're more expensive than visiting a doctor's office.[14]

If you're in graduate or professional school, the university health service may be an option for you to use. It's likely to be convenient and covered through school health insurance if you have it. An additional health care option can sometimes be found in communities where medical or dental schools are located. Some medical centers have a clinic type of private practice facility for attending physicians who also teach and supervise medical students and residents. Others have clinics with supervised residents and interns.[15]

You're best served by developing a relationship with a physician whom you like and trust and who can come to know you and your physical condition. Doctors are more likely to recognize changes if they've seen you regularly over an extended period of time.

Your Primary Care Physician

"Are you one of the doctor's patients?" the receptionist always asks. "No, but I need to be." If you wait until you desperately need medical care to find a doctor for the first time, you'll be incredibly frustrated. I prefer to find a doctor first then meet her or him by making an appointment and giving him or her a copy of my medical history. Then when I need help, I can tell the receptionist, "Yes, I'm a patient," and not feel like a stranger in a strange land. It's important to have a primary care physician, usually a family practice physician or an internist. Your primary care physician will handle most of your medical problems and refer you to specialists if necessary. She or he provides you with comprehensive medical care, offers advice on how to stay well, and serves as your health advocate, coordinating all of your care.[16]

How do you find a primary care physician? You'll have to start with any limits placed on your options by your particular health plan. Then ask around. Who do your coworkers use and like? Ask people you feel some identification with. A coworker who comes from a very different economic level, or someone with lots of kids (if you don't have any) may have different priorities in looking for medical care. If you would prefer someone who is understanding of your religious practices, sexual orientation, or size, ask for suggestions from people who you sense are also sensitive to those issues. Perhaps the doctors at your college health center can refer you to someone in your new area. Or maybe your alumni association can direct you to alumni in the place where you relocate. Local hospitals often have physician referral services.

For a crisis or an emergency you may be more concerned about finding the best technical person for the job, regardless of his or her interpersonal skills. The arrogant but brilliant surgeons portrayed on TV programs such as *Chicago Hope* and *ER* are good examples of this. For ongoing care, however, both technical skill and interpersonal style are important to consider.

You are entitled to health care providers you are comfortable with and who take the time to listen to you and answer your questions. Use an initial visit to evaluate the physician. How do you feel in the office? How long do you have to wait to see her or him? How do the office staff treat you? [17]

During a first visit a doctor should get a thorough medical history from you. Is this someone you can discuss personal concerns with? Is she or he condescending to you, or do you feel he or she is genuinely concerned about your well-being and treats you with respect? Is this someone you can place your trust in—someone who will work *with* you to manage your health care? [18]

Talk with the physician about his or her approach to health care. So-called aggressive doctors generally intervene early and vigorously if there's a problem. They order tests to get information and make a diagnosis and are more likely to recommend corrective measures quickly. More conservative doctors prefer to wait a while before intervening in this way. They believe that many problems will resolve themselves with time either by disappearing or by more clearly defining themselves on their own. More conservative doctors usually recommend simpler procedures first when they intervene. [19] You need to decide which general approach is more consistent with what you like in a doctor who treats you.

During a first visit you should also get some procedural questions answered. What hospitals is the doctor affiliated with? Will she or he take and return phone calls? Will the office staff file insurance claims, or do you need to do that on your own? Will the doctor accept your insurance reimbursement as payment in full? [20]

Whenever you see your primary care physician for a problem, be prepared. Present your concern clearly and concisely, and explain what's been going on and for how long. The doctor will probably ask you some specific questions, so be prepared to present the details required (Is the pain sharp or dull? Is it worse at some times of the day? On an empty stomach?). Take notes as you talk to the doctor, and ask questions if there's anything you don't understand.

Your Rights as a Patient

One young M.D. advises that you shouldn't be afraid to stand up to physicians if you feel they're talking down to you or not listening to you in a respectful way. "I've found," he says, "that many physicians, when told that, actually come around and respond."

You have a right to confidentiality, to your dignity, to know what's being done and why, and to be part of the decision-making process about your own health care and treatment. Know what you're going to the health care provider for, and read about your symptoms. The provider will have the medical and technical knowledge and expertise. She or he should present you with information about the diagnosis of your problem, how it can be investigated, the prognosis (what's likely to happen over time), and your treatment alternatives. *You* have the knowledge and expertise on issues of personal comfort, risk, and cost. You have the right to decide among the alternatives presented. How much discomfort are you able to deal with? How much risk are you willing to take? How much expense can you afford? If you don't understand the doctor's medical explanation, speak up and say so. Ask him or her to explain it in terms you understand.[21]

If the doctor prescribes a medication, you have a right to be fully informed about that drug. What is the name of the drug, and what is it supposed to do? How will it help you, and how likely is it to cure the illness or eliminate the symptoms? Ask how the drug works, how you'll know whether it's working, how long you'll have to take it, and how long it should be until you see or feel its effects. Are there possible side effects and risks? What should you do if you experience them? How and when should the drug be taken? Are there any foods, drinks, or activities that should be avoided while you're using the drug? Does the medication come in more than one form (for example, if the prescription is for a capsule too large for you to swallow, is there a liquid form)?[22]

Ask your doctor if she or he can give you any samples of the medication to try out before you fill a prescription. You can also ask whether there is a generic brand of the drug available that will be less expensive and whether the generic brand is really equivalent to the name brand. Is it absorbed by the body at the same rate?[23]

You have a right to ask about alternatives to this medication. Are there other medications that are more likely to work, less likely to cause unpleasant side effects, or less costly? Are there treatments other than medication for your condition? What's the risk of waiting without treatment for a while?[24]

Use medication when the benefits to be derived outweigh any potential risks. Make sure the recommended medication is the best alternative available for treating your condition. For example, if you need to lower your cholesterol, could you try changing your diet and exercise habits first rather than immediately beginning daily medication? Finally, use any prescribed medication *properly.* If the doctor says, for example, to take it until you finish the bottle even if you feel better, finish the bottle. If the directions are to take it on an empty stomach, do so.[25]

Your health care provider may recommend some tests in order to gather information to make a diagnosis or rule something out. Testing shouldn't be done unnecessarily or excessively. Some tests can be done in the provider's office and others only in special facilities with specifically trained personnel.[26] You have the right to have all your questions answered before agreeing to any test. Why should the test be done? What will it reveal about your condition that isn't already known, and how will the test result change the way your case is being handled? What does the test cost, and will your insurance cover all or part of it? Discuss candidly the potential risks or side effects and any alternatives there are to your taking the test. You can ask the doctor to describe exactly how the test is done and what degree of pain or discomfort is involved both during the test and afterward.[27]

Patient rights are specified in a number of ways, but we often aren't aware that they're so clearly spelled out and there for us to claim. The *doctrine of informed consent,* for example, recognizes the patient's right to be informed about her or his condition and the physician's duty to explain to the patient the proposed course of action, the risks involved,

plausible alternatives (including nontreatment), and their risks and benefits.[28]

If you are treated in a hospital, ask if they have a *patient's bill of rights,* and if so, read it. This document gives the patient and his or her family the right to complete information about diagnosis, treatment, and prognosis explained in understandable language.[29]

A *durable power of attorney* for health care, signed when you're competent, enables you to name someone to make your health care decisions for you in the event that you can't. This responsibility should be given to someone who understands your values, beliefs, and wishes in regard to your health and treatment. If you don't legally designate someone to make these decisions for you, the hospital or doctors will do so. You can consult a lawyer to write a durable power of attorney or request a form from the social services department at a hospital.[30]

A *living will* claims the right of a terminally ill adult to instruct physicians and hospital staff to withhold or with-

draw life sustaining procedures if medical judgments con-
clude that the patient will never be able to function independently. A living will must be prepared in advance, when
you're mentally competent to make the choices involved, and
it should conform to the laws in your state. You can get the
appropriate forms from the local medical society, the social
services department of the hospital, or a lawyer. Include a
copy of the living will in your medical records, and give
copies to family members and perhaps to close friends. Be
sure your doctors and your family understand your wishes as
documented in the living will.[31]

Taking Care of Yourself

> Some people, especially men, wait until they're near death before
> they'll see a doctor. Don't wait.   —W.M., nurse practitioner

According to recent surveys, in nine out of ten cases,
Americans take care of their own everyday health problems
without going to a professional.[32] There is much you can do
for yourself, by yourself, to monitor your own health. Used
properly, easily accessible tools such as the blood pressure
machines in malls and drugstores, home cholesterol measure-
ment kits, and home pregnancy tests can help you recognize
changes in your health condition. The National Health Information Center (1-800-336-4797) can refer you to organizations best able to answer particular questions you have. A
good medical guide can also help you monitor many problems and determine when a call or a visit to the doctor is

necessary. *None of these, however, is a substitute for seeing a doctor when needed.*

Basic first aid supplies and personal care equipment, such as the items listed below, can be kept in your own home.[33]

Thermometer
Tweezers
Heating pad
Alcohol
An antidiarrhea agent such as Kaopectate
Antacid
A mild, nonstinging antiseptic
Aspirin or aspirin substitute
Spirits of ammonia
Band-Aids in various sizes
Cotton-tipped applicators or cotton balls
Adhesive tape
Scissors
Sterile gauze pads
Petroleum jelly
Hydrogen peroxide
Syrup of ipecac (to induce vomiting in case of accidental
    poisoning)
Calamine lotion
Activated charcoal (helpful for gas)

If you use over-the-counter drugs, use them safely and effectively. Read the label carefully and follow the instructions provided, including how much to take, how often to take it, the maximum dosage per day, and the method for taking it (for example, chew two tablets after each meal).

Check out the list of active ingredients. Are there any that you're allergic to or that are already contained in another product you're taking at the same time? Note any warnings about possible side effects, people who shouldn't take the drug if they have specific medical conditions, and when to stop using the product. Note drug interaction precautions and the expiration date, after which the drug won't be as effective or could be dangerous. If you buy an over-the-counter drug from a pharmacist, ask her or him about the product. If you still have questions, talk to a doctor.[34]

The American Medical Association recommends a checkup every five years if you're healthy and under forty years old.[35] While the frequency of screening examinations should be determined by each individual in consultation with his or her health care provider, several regular screenings are suggested for younger adults. Women should have an annual PAP smear beginning at age eighteen or when they become sexually active. Physicians may suggest less frequent PAP smears after a number of normal results. Blood pressure, for both men and women, should be taken every two years if it remains in the normal range, more frequently if not. Cholesterol should be checked every five years for adults over twenty.[36]

I stopped going [to the dentist] because I didn't trust him. For one thing, he wore an outfit that buttoned on the side, the kind spaceship crews wear in low-budget science fiction movies. For another thing, he and his cohorts *always left the room* when they X-rayed me. They'd make up flimsy excuses, like "I have to go

put my socks in the dryer," or "I think the cat is throwing up."
Then they'd flip the X-ray switch and race out of the room,
probably to a lead-lined concrete bunker.

—Dave Barry, "Dentistry Self-Drilled" [37]

Despite what Dave Barry says, regular dental care is important. Minor problems can be caught before they become major ones. Even a simple cleaning can become an ordeal if you wait three years rather than having it done every six months. Select a dentist with the same care you do a doctor. Get recommendations from friends. You can also consult the American Dental Association Directory or your state or local dental society. [38] When you start with a new dentist, bring with you, or have sent, any X rays from your previous dentist.

Mental health care is also important. Some of the popular magazines have published stress tests that list possible changes in your life and give you points for each. You add your total to get an indication of how much stress you may experience. The chain of changes that accompany graduation—change in your role, starting a new job or graduate school, change in relationships, and so forth—can often create major stress. There are a number of preventive habits you can develop to maintain good health in unhealthy times and situations. [39]

- Don't smoke
- Maintain a smoke-free environment
- Keep your blood cholesterol under two hundred
- Exercise regularly

- Get enough sleep
- Limit your alcohol intake
- Avoid excessive exposure to the sun

Some stress may manifest itself in physical ways such as headaches, fatigue, or a persistent cold. Other times you may feel depressed or overwhelmed. Some HMOs offer educational programs or counseling services. If you're on your own, seek out some professional counseling if you think it will help you get over the hurdle. The options may not be as easily accessible or as readily affordable as simply going to the counseling center on campus, but there are counseling resources in most communities. Sometimes just being able to talk with others who are going through some of the same changes, or have done so recently, can provide needed support and reassurance.

SEVEN

Ain't No Mountain High Enough: Graduate and Professional School

Some college graduates head right out into the job market and begin their careers, or at least start working, as soon as possible. Others decide, for a variety of reasons, to continue their education. For some, an advanced degree is needed before they feel they can pursue the career they're interested in. Others may be looking at graduate or professional school (law school, medical school, business school) because that's always been the plan, or because their parents or professors have urged them in that direction. There's a stereotype that some people are perpetual students—choosing to live a familiar lifestyle as long as they can. The decision to go to graduate or professional school should be just that—a decision rather than a reflex or winner by default. The more clear you are about your goals and reasons for being in graduate or professional school, the better chance you have of selecting the right one and making the most of the experience.

Starting Early

Your choice of courses throughout college will help prepare you for the graduate school experience. Seek out an academic advisor who is both experienced and understanding. She or he should help you evaluate your strengths and weaknesses and develop a reasonable academic schedule, especially for your freshman year.[1] Challenge yourself by taking classes that require papers, presentations, and seminar-type discussions. These will be more rigorous and take more preparation on your part, but so will graduate school. Become familiar with this kind of academic approach. It will prepare you more for the kind of work that will be expected of you in graduate or professional school.

With so many graduate programs and professional schools to explore, start collecting information early in your college career. Faculty members are rich sources of information about their own graduate programs and graduate student experiences. Many will have contacts in professional networks that put them in touch with graduates of other programs and faculty members at a variety of schools. Bear in mind, however, that schools and programs change over time. It can take as little as one professor retiring or leaving to alter the tone and focus of a program. It's important, therefore, to check out the current situation at any school you're considering.

Another approach to collecting information is to contact people who have written books, magazine or newspaper articles, journal articles, or professional papers about topics that interest you. Write them a letter and tell them you enjoyed reading their work. See if they're currently teaching at a college or university with a graduate program. Often their affiliation is noted in the author's biography that accompanies any written material. Tell them what your areas of interest are, and ask if they can suggest some good graduate programs for you to look into.

I tried this approach the second time I applied to graduate schools, and I was amazed at the number of responses I received. Several of the same programs were recommended by a number of people, and some of them even suggested particular faculty members for me to contact at those schools. I established contact with a faculty member at one institution who encouraged me to apply there, offered to be my advisor if I was accepted, and told that to the graduate student admissions committee that interviewed me. He became my mentor before I arrived and continued to support and challenge me throughout my graduate school career.

Most Ph.D. programs require a commitment to research. Take advantage of opportunities to do research during your undergraduate years. Some schools sponsor research institutes that encourage independent projects or collaborative efforts between students and faculty. If you're at a university that has graduate programs, some graduate students use undergraduate assistants to help with their research. Faculty members often look for research assistants to work with them. They may even be able to hire you as an assistant, using grant funds. If they don't, you can still volunteer to help. As an undergraduate, one young woman was listed as the junior author of a professional journal article about research she had assisted her faculty mentor with throughout her four years of college. She thus brought a proven research track record to her graduate school applications.

Some professors offer academic credit for your contributions—perhaps as independent study or as part of a course you're taking with them. If you don't have to earn a lot of money every summer, look for summer research opportunities. Even if they don't pay much, you might at least get room and board, and you can work at a part-time job such as lifeguard or waiter to fill in your finances. Research experience will help you with your graduate school research requirements, and it will also make your application stand out in the selection process. Cultivate faculty contacts in your field of interest. This will improve the quality of the reference letters they write for you. Someone familiar with your written work, research capabilities, and intellectual curiosity can write a better reference on your behalf.

If you work part time or do community service work, consider opportunities that relate to your chosen field. If you're interested in medical school, for example, try volunteering or working at a hospital; if you're intrigued by the prospect of law school, work with a legal aid program. This is a good way to take a trip across some potential transition bridges and see if where your graduate degree would take you is where you really want to go. Experience the world of work. It can give your graduate or professional school experience a broader perspective.

Be careful, however, of becoming so focused toward graduate or professional school that you limit your entire undergraduate experience. You'll be focused soon enough. One medical school graduate suggests, for example, taking advantage of nonscience courses while you can. Your extracurricular activities during college will also show a graduate admissions committee that you made time to do more than just take classes. Activities could relate to your academic field (for example, volunteering at an AIDS group home), but they don't have to. A broader range of interests can also work in your favor. Any activities that demonstrate successful interactions with people are a plus.[2] Most graduate and professional schools look at your overall record—good undergraduate grades, high graduate or professional school admission test scores, strong communication skills, quantitative and analytical skills, work experience, extracurricular activities, and motivation.[3] According to one premedical advisor, medical schools emphasize the first two—grades (especially science grades) and MCATs.

You'll need to decide when to take the appropriate graduate or professional school admissions test (GRE, MCAT, LSAT, GMAT, for example). Booklets that describe each test, provide application materials, and give sample questions are available at your college career development office or by contacting the appropriate test publisher:

- Graduate Record Examination
  Educational Testing Service
  P.O. Box 6000
  Princeton, NJ 08541-6000
  609-771-7670
- Law School Admission Council
  Law Services
  661 Penn Street
  Newtown, PA 18940-0998
  215-968-1001

- Graduate Management Admission Test (for MBA programs)
  Educational Testing Service
  P.O. Box 6103
  Princeton, NJ 08541-6103
  609-771-7330
  Internet: gopher.ets.org.
- Medical College Admission Test Program Office
  P.O. Box 4056
  Iowa City, IA 52243
  319-337-1357

If you have a documented disability and require particular accommodations for taking the test, there is a form you can send along with your test application to arrange for those accommodations to be reasonably met.

If you take your graduate or professional school admission test in the spring of your junior year, you can retake it in the fall of your senior year if you're not satisfied with your score. By taking it in your junior year you can also be sure of meeting any early fall application deadlines. The disadvantage of taking it early is that it can be hard to prepare while you're also taking a full academic load of classes. Consider taking a lighter load, perhaps making up the credits during the summer, if you choose the junior year testing option. If you take the test in the fall of your senior year, you can study over the summer.[4]

Senior Year

Some colleges offer senior year academic experiences that provide a capstone to academic majors and also offer good preparation for graduate or professional school. One graduate, for example, describes how his intense last-semester honors program gave him the confidence that he was ready for anything. The two weeks of honors exams and orals, using outside examiners, was much closer to a graduate school experience than to a traditional undergraduate one.

Graduate or professional school is more productive and enjoyable if you know why you're going—what you want to get out of it and where you hope it will take you. Explore your goals with faculty, family, friends, and alumni who have already headed across that same bridge. Encourage them to push you and give you a hard time. You should be able to clearly articulate your motives. As uncomfortable as it can feel to have to explain or defend your choices, the process can really help you get the focus needed. This can also serve as a practice interview to prepare you for the real thing. This process can raise questions about whether graduate or professional school is the right step for you at this point. If you have doubts, you're better off addressing them now, rather than committing yourself to a graduate program and having doubts after you're there.

Learn as much as you can about your prospective graduate or professional school interests and where they can lead. Some colleges bring in speakers to talk to seniors about different careers and graduate programs. Others will be willing to put you in touch with alumni.

The senior year is also the time to write your graduate school applications. This means narrowing your choices and completing the application process. It will take time and planning to write essays on, for example, your philosophy of education, why you want to go into law, where you see yourself in ten years; take admission tests if you've planned them for this fall; interview; and so forth. Build this task into your senior year schedule and start early. Use faculty and staff advisors on your campus to help you. Many schools designate specific faculty members as premed and prelaw advisors. Career development offices also offer information and assistance.

Some professional and graduate schools use common application services. You can submit all your application information to such a service, and it will forward what's required to the schools you designate that subscribe to that service. Ask the schools you're applying to whether they use a common application.

Answer graduate or professional school application questions directly. Don't pretend to know more than you do; your application will be read by those who know the field better than you do. Discuss original or independent work you've done, and talk about extracurricular activities that have developed skills related to the program you're applying to. If an application asks you for personal comments about anything else you want the admissions committee to know, take the opportunity seriously. This is your chance to express who you are, how you're different, why you want to study in this area, and what you bring with you. Have friends and professors read over your essays and give you feedback, and *always* double-check spelling and grammar.[5]

In some fields you will have to decide whether to apply for a master's degree program or a doctoral program. There are pros and cons of each. If you're hoping to eventually teach at the college level, a Ph.D. is important. Whether to apply for that longer program immediately is another question. Take time to look at the kinds of jobs you eventually hope to do. Check with your career development office to explore all the options. You may not be aware of *all* the possibilities until you do some research. If you don't need a Ph.D. to do what you want to do, getting one could overqualify you for jobs you really want to hold. On the other hand, if your goals are clear and you can commit yourself for four to seven years, you may decide to go directly into a Ph.D. program and complete your degree as soon as possible.

A master's program will often qualify you for the jobs you want, or at least the entry level of those jobs. You can also always consider Ph.D. programs down the road, after you've worked a few years. Your focus may undergo some changes, and this added time and experience could point you in a somewhat different direction for the more advanced degree. Some graduates who initially expect to go for their Ph.D.'s opt instead for master's degrees first. They then start working and discover they enjoy what they are doing and are advancing in a good direction, even though it is different from what they'd originally planned. They wind up perfectly satisfied with what they are able to do with a master's degree.

As you narrow your choices, look closely at the schools you're considering. Consult books such as *Medical School Admissions Requirements,* published by the Association of American Medical Colleges. This book provides information about the types of applicants each school tends to accept.[6] An Internet search through Netscape can let you browse through information about various graduate and professional schools, financial aid available, and so forth. If at all possible, visit and talk to both faculty members and current students. Schools and programs vary greatly. You want to feel comfortable with both the faculty and the students and also happy with what you're doing and how you're treated. Prioritize what's important to you before you make your decision where to go.

Exercise: Graduate School Bingo

Imagine yourself as a student in your ideal graduate or professional school (medical, law, business, dental, etc.).

1. Where is it located and in what kind of setting? _____

_____

2. If it's part of a larger university, how integrated is it with other professional and/or undergraduate schools? _____

_____

3. How large is the graduate school? _____

_____

4. How many students are in your program, and what are they like? _____

_____

5. If you talk to students, how would they describe their experiences? _____

_____

6. What's the focus or orientation of the program (quantitative or research oriented, theoretical, hands-on practical, a combination)? _____

_____

7. What requirements, if any, are there in your program? __

_____

8. Is there a minimum course load you have to take each semester and/or a time period within which you have to complete your degree? _____

_____

9. What are the courses like (for example, what do the class syllabi look like)? _____

_____

10. What opportunities are there for practical experiences (clinical work in med school, practicums in a psychology program)? _____

_____

11. How are graduate students treated by faculty, and how accessible are the professors? _____

_____

12. How competitive is the environment, and how comfortable do you feel there? _____

_____

13. What kinds of opportunities are there to do independent research or work? _____

_____

Now prioritize these qualities.

1. Essential in any program you attend

_____

_____

_____

_____

_____

2. Would be nice, but not crucial

_____

_____

_____

_____

_____

3. Not very important

_____

_____

_____

_____

_____

Your narrowing process should include a good look at the faculty—the people you will learn from and study with. These individuals will shape the form of your educational experience and can also affect your entry into the professional world. Who are the faculty members in each program? Will they be there when you are (are any going on sabbatical, close to retirement, or planning to leave for other reasons)? What are their research and teaching interests, and how much contact will you have with them? Personal contact, if you visit, is the best way to really get a feel for how they relate to you. Call ahead and schedule appointments with faculty you want to talk with if you visit for an interview.

Try to figure out what you will get at each program and what the program expects of you. If you're a woman or person of color in a field where you'll be in the minority, look at sources of encouragement and support at the school and in the program. For example, some schools have women's interest groups or organizations for students of color. Graduate student associations often serve as advocates on campus for the needs of graduate students.

Finding Financial Aid

Financial aid can also play a role in choosing a graduate or professional school. Most graduate school money is decentralized. There is no single financial aid form to fill out to access all funds, so you'll need to apply directly to a number of sources for aid.[7] Contact the graduate schools you're applying to and find out what forms they require.

While there is little federal grant money available for graduate study, there is a significant amount of loan money. Need is calculated based on the difference between expected family contribution and the cost of the school. As a graduate, you can qualify as an independent student so that your expected family income will be based solely on your own income and assets. To assure that your independent status isn't questioned, make sure you're not claimed as a tax exemption on your parents' income tax return for the calendar year just before the year for which you're seeking an award (for example, the 1995 tax return for a 1996–97 award).[8] If you already have outstanding college loans, consider the advisability of adding further debt right away. For example, if you take out a ten-thousand-dollar federal loan that gets paid back at 5 percent interest over ten years, that will cost you about $106 a month, every month, for ten years (a loan at 8 percent interest requires a monthly payment of $121 a month).[9] Add that to undergraduate loan repayments, rent, utilities, and possibly car payments, and those expenses can eat up a monthly paycheck quickly.

There are other potential sources of financial aid. A number of states make help available to residents of that state who attend graduate or professional school in the state. They may, however, be limited to specific areas of study or population groups.[10]

Consult your financial aid office about scholarships and fellowships that are awarded on a national basis rather than for a specific school. Some examples are National Science Foundation Fellowships, National Research Council Fellowships, Mellon Fellowships, Goldwater Scholarships, Rhodes Scholarships, British Marshall Scholarships, Truman Fellowships, and Fulbright Fellowships). If you're awarded one of these scholarships or fellowships, you may be an even more attractive candidate to some of the schools you're applying to.

Finally, explore all possibilities at the graduate or professional schools themselves. When you request applications, write to the departmental office of the program you're applying to as well as to the graduate admissions and financial aid offices. Ask specifically about university-administered financial aid resources. Possibilities include departmental grants, research assistantships, internships, jobs, and teaching assistantships. Many of these will provide tuition or stipends of various amounts, or both, or at least waive of out-of-state tuition. You're not likely to find out about all of these options unless you specifically ask.[11] Ask early because once the available funds are gone for the year, they're gone.

My experiences as a graduate student at two different institutions reflect the variety of sources to be tapped. As a graduate fresh out of college I entered a master's degree program at the graduate school of education of a major university. I had not applied for financial aid, but once I arrived I decided to check out the possibilities for future semesters. I had no idea what I might qualify for, but I went to the office of the dean of the graduate school of education to inquire. I was amazed when they said, "We think we can come up with something." They did. They immediately offered me an assistantship in one of the offices at the school working on an educational research project. It was a wonderful experience and also provided a waiver of my tuition costs.

Five years later, after getting my master's degree and working for several years, I prepared to enter a Ph.D. program in education at a large midwestern university. This time I inquired about scholarships and assistantships during the application process. I interviewed for, and was offered, a teaching assistantship in the introductory course for education majors at the university. This assistantship provided me with in-state tuition and a livable stipend. The course also employed more than twenty teaching assistants from various programs in the school of education. As a person moving a long distance to a new part of the country, I thus found a way to immediately get to know people I had something in common with—a ready-made social circle. Many of my closest friends in graduate school came from this group of T.A.'s and others I met through them.

At some schools, graduate and professional students can earn room, board, and a stipend by holding resident advisor assistantships. If you're an R.A. in college, you should be well qualified for one of these. You may, however, also be tired of living in a residence hall with staff responsibilities, so don't necessarily jump at this option too quickly.

If you have more than one loan to pay off after you finish graduate school, consider consolidating all those loans into one at the lowest interest rate. Consult with a trusted expert at your school or through your current lending institution about how to do this. *Don't* consolidate loans before you finish grad school, however, or you will lose any deferment privileges you have on undergraduate loans.

Alternatives to Starting Graduate School Right Away

> Don't assume you have to go directly to grad school from college. Most of the people I know in grad school now who went straight through without taking time off are having some doubts about what they're doing. It's easier to take time off before starting grad school than to take time off or a leave of absence after you start. You may not come back.   —M.S.

A big decision is whether to go straight on to graduate or professional school or to take some time to work or travel first. Some graduates find it eases the transition to go right on to grad school. Your student habits and student style are well honed, and you may feel like you're "on a roll." One graduate described how going directly to grad school made the transition to adulthood much easier because that student aspect of her life remained constant while so many other aspects were changing. Another found that while he didn't exactly love law school, he did like still being in school rather than working nine to five. He also liked having some free time between classes, a gym to use on campus, a social circle, and the freedom to still blow off a class once in a while.

Others recommend taking a few years to work, travel, or

do other things before heading off to graduate or professional school. One young man used the time between college and grad school as a "pit stop in reality." "It can help you, be more sure if you really want to go there," he says. Besides serving as a reality check, taking time off can give you a chance to make some money to offset the cost of graduate school and pay off undergraduate loans. Some graduate schools also like to see some work or real-life experience on applications.

> Graduate school isn't the "real world" by any stretch of the imagination, and a lot of people in it don't have a concept of how the real world works. I know grad students who don't know how to write a check! Get some life experience.   —M.S.

If you wait too long to return, however, the transition back can be more difficult. You could have to retrain yourself into effective study patterns and struggle to get back into the classroom/papers/test mode. Your confidence may waver if this adaptation feels too great. Keep your toe in the academic pool by occasionally taking a single course or perhaps a workshop during the summer.

Another alternative, acceptable at many graduate and professional schools, is to apply for admission and, if you're accepted, defer your enrollment for a year. This will give you time before beginning but also guarantee you a place and minimize the possibility that you'll never go back.

You can also combine work with part-time graduate or professional courses for a year or two before focusing full time on a degree program. Some employers will help pay your tuition if you're in a program related to your job and if you agree to work for them for a certain amount of time after you complete your degree.

Some graduates enter alternative programs to law or medical school, such as paralegal training or physician's assistant programs. These move them into the professional field of their choice but in a somewhat different capacity. Physician's assistant programs, for example, prepare you to perform a wide range of medical duties from basic primary care to specialty procedures, as long as you're under the supervision of a licensed physician.[12] Some who enter alternative programs eventually go on to law or medical school. Others find themselves quite happy with where their first degree takes them.

Another alternative, for those interested in medical school but lacking the depth of undergraduate science experience, is the medical postbaccalaureate program offered at a number of colleges. These programs offer a one-year concentrated science program in preparation for medical school.

Making the Transition

> It was a wonderful time. I was taking classes I wanted and loved with people who were into the same things I was. We had all these wacky and intellectual conversations.   —C.C.

Graduate or professional school can be very different from undergraduate school. If you go simply expecting more of the same, you may be surprised. If you go expecting nirvana, you may be disappointed. "What was most surprising to me about life after college," says one graduate, "was how much I hated grad school."

In graduate school you're on your own. I remember sitting in my new apartment in Philadelphia shortly after I'd moved there to start a master's program in counseling. I was used to living in residence halls where notices got posted every day and where there was always someone around to remind us about deadlines and forms and what was going on. Well, one day I found myself wondering how I'd know when to register for my classes. I searched out my catalog and fall semester schedule booklet, and as I looked through them I realized that I (and every other first-year graduate student whose last name began with S–Z) was supposed to be at the school registering that afternoon. That was my first big clue that I "wasn't in Kansas anymore."

In graduate school expectations aren't always clearly stated. Perhaps you won't be required, for example, to attend a talk or a guest lecture on campus, but your professor might expect you to go. Keep up with current professional journals in the library. This may also be an unwritten expectation.

Graduate or professional study is generally more difficult, more intense, and more focused. That can be exciting and stimulating, or it can be trying if you're in the wrong place or not ready for that intensity. Some programs give you more flexibility and freedom than you've known before in an academic setting, especially if you're coming from a more structured and rigid undergraduate program. You may find faculty treating you differently. One graduate described how her graduate school professors were much more willing than her teachers in college to sit and talk with her and work with her on what she wanted to do. Some graduates, on the other hand, describe their transition from undergraduate school to professional school as going from a more creative, flexible life to a "boot camp" atmosphere with a lot more structure and limits.

The pace in professional schools is also different from that in undergraduate programs. One medical school graduate describes having a much heavier workload and a lot more exams with fewer time-outs. "Often," he says, "there was an exam in some course every two weeks and quizzes every week." More courses may be offered pass/fail, and unless there's a disguised pass/fail system that everybody knows equates with traditional A–F letter grades (for example, high honors, honors, pass, low pass, fail), it can be disorienting not to have an ongoing indication of how you're doing.

In some professional schools, your entire grade is based on comprehensive exams at the end of a term or even an entire academic year. For someone used to more frequent feedback, this can be frustrating. Practice exams and working with a study group can fill some of these gaps. The movie *The Paper Chase* depicts the stressful first year of law school for a group of new students who live through it with varying degrees of success.

If you're in a Ph.D. program, the doctoral dissertation is always looming in front of you. It takes incredible focus and perseverance to get it done. Start thinking about research possibilities early. Your professors will have particular areas of research, perhaps offshoots of their own projects, that they'd like to see someone else pursue. Also, keep in touch with your former professors from undergraduate school. They will probably be interested in your progress, and they can also be good sources of ideas and contacts as you develop your professional direction.

The People

> There were different types of people in my classes. Not all "like me." I was the youngest in my program in grad school. People with more experiences contributed a lot to class.   —C.T.

The student population in graduate and professional school is quite different from that in undergraduate school. Many students here are older or have families or work, or all of the above. They're not necessarily there to meet people but primarily to study and get their degrees. Often graduate students find less cohesion and support and fewer people just hanging out together as they did in college.

Some programs, however, make a real effort to encourage camaraderie, especially among the incoming class each year. Those relationships often persist throughout the program. The size and makeup of your entering graduate or professional school class is thus pretty important. In graduate school your friends generally come from your classes, and your classes are predominantly made up of the people in your program. This can create a ready-made social system. The good part of this is that you're all going through the same experiences together. The bad part is that you're all going through the same experiences together! Your schedules will be similar, and you can, for example, study together and celebrate as a group after the big exam. But you may get tired of working and playing with all the same people all the time.

Graduate schools are often separated from the larger university, and even if you're at a big school, you may feel as if your world is really quite small. When I went to a large university, I really only considered the graduate school of education building to be "my school." I didn't identify much with the rest of the campus.

This small-world feeling may be something you enjoy. But if it feels a bit too insulated to you, there are things you can do to broaden your world. Keep up with a hobby, an interest, or a relationship to maintain some balance in your life. Push yourself to get out to activities or events that interest you both on campus and in the community. This will give you a chance to meet people with similar interests outside your program.

Your choice of living situation can also influence the scope of your world. A law school dorm, for example, will give you close proximity to people in your classes and those ahead of you. This can be helpful for studying, but it might also be too much law too much of the time. A general graduate dorm will enable you to meet other grad students from a variety of different programs. If you're relocating somewhere new by yourself, starting off in a graduate dorm could help you begin to meet people. You can always move to your own place after the first semester or year.

Another living option is to share an apartment or a house. Sometimes groups of students from a program get a place together. Or perhaps you have friends from your undergraduate school, or a cousin, or a friend of a friend who will also be living in the area and who might live with you. If you share a place with someone outside of your program, it can expand your circle of acquaintances and friends. When I was in graduate school the first time, in a counseling psychology program, my best living situation was sharing an apartment with a woman who was in a graduate program in communications. She was also interested in psychology, and I was interested in the film work she was doing. We each enjoyed meeting the other's friends—people we wouldn't have met if we hadn't known each other.

You can also share a living space with someone who isn't a student at all. This will give you a look at life in the real world. One disadvantage of this shared living situation is that you may be on different types of schedules. For example, perhaps one of you has to be up early every morning to commute to work, while the other stays up late every night to study.

Graduate or professional school can open up many exciting paths. Take advantage of summer and vacation opportunities for jobs, internships, and other practical experiences. These will give you valuable experience, opportunities to meet people in your future field, and a chance to do interesting and often important work.

E I G H T

Do You Know Where You're Going To? The Career Path and Alternatives

It's important to do your homework and talk with everyone—you never know where opportunities lie. Always have your résumé ready and updated and always be able to tell a "story" about yourself and your experiences. Everything you've accomplished and done is valuable. You'd be surprised at how each experience has led you to the next whether you realized it at the time or not.   —R.C.

One graduate describes a job as something to tide you over and a career as what you want to do with your life. An experienced career counselor suggests that some choices may feel as though they move you off of your original path. If you look hard enough, however, you can probably find some thread or connection that links them. Often these connections won't be apparent until years later when you look back at the path you have taken. The first step may be a transition across a bridge that leads you to someplace new. You may stay there, or find that this new place leads you to another bridge, that leads you to someplace else, that leads you to another bridge, and so forth. You have to cross that first bridge, however, to begin.

Catherine's Story

Catherine describes herself as having "sort of fallen into" a career path. "It really was not at all what I intended to do," she says, "but I think it's where I belong." Catherine was a science major at a small liberal arts college. Her original plans were to go to graduate school, get a Ph.D., and eventually teach or do research at the college level. Medical problems during her senior year of college required her to take an academic overload in order to graduate on time. Catherine decided not to worry about grad school right away, and instead she took a year off to work before continuing in her planned career direction. Catherine wanted to stay in the area. She had a summer job lined up at her college, and she was able to look for a job for the upcoming year during that time.

For that first job, Catherine says she literally fell into a position as a high school science teacher at an all-girl Catholic high school. "I really didn't enjoy it very much," she says, "but it turned out that the school closed down by merging with another at the end of that year, so I was out of a job again."

Catherine's next step was to take a job as a biology lab technician back at her former college. She stayed for two years while also taking education courses to qualify for a teaching certificate. While working and studying, Catherine kept looking into what she really wanted to do. She continued to make use of the resources available to her through her college career development office. Catherine realized that where she'd had the most fun, during her undergraduate years, was working part-time at the city's science center in its children's program. She decided that what she really wanted to do was to work with younger kids, not the college population she'd originally intended to work with.

Catherine went out to do some information interviews to find out just what she would need in order to teach younger kids, and she wound up getting offered a job through one of those interviews. They were looking for an elementary-level science person with some background, and Catherine had accumulated that background through her part-time work at the science center and her year at the high school. "I was in the right place at the right time," she says, "and I love what I'm doing." Catherine's work experience and persistent efforts to focus on what she really wanted to do paid off.

Justin's Story

Justin graduated second in his class from a branch of his state university. He majored in theater and English literature. Right after graduation Justin worked in a bookstore he'd been working in all through college. He didn't actively pursue a career direction right away, but "sort of waited to see what happened." When he started to look for jobs, he sent résumés to places that were related to his field of interest but had no luck.

Justin began to get desperate, and one friend set up an interview for him for a receptionist position at the place where she worked. He soon realized, however, that the qualities they were looking for weren't his strengths. Justin looked through the employment ads in the newspaper but didn't find positions that he felt fit him.

Finally he decided to try a temp agency. He made a high score on their basic skills tests, and the agency took him on. Justin was a college graduate with close to a 4.0 GPA, a year's study abroad, and bilingual skills. His first temporary job assignment was to sit in a parking lot for seventeen hours counting cars every hour on the hour for $6.25 an hour. The second job he was sent on was to assemble training manuals. Next he was sent to a bank to do basic data processing.

Justin was a fast and accurate worker. He believes that his work ethic, effort on every job, and persistent requests for more challenging work paid off with the temp agency. They finally sent him to a life insurance company where he started to work with computers and finances. He worked with a complex computer system that required a lot of problem-solving ability. Justin enjoyed what he was doing because it was challenging and he had to use his brain.

After four months as a temp at this company, Justin became a permanent employee there. He proved his value through his hard work and performance on the job. He learned that you need to have some experience in a company before you can move up. You don't come right out of college to an executive position. Justin used some of his college skills in this job by writing parts of the manual for the computer system. He also nurtured his interest in theater by acting in community theater productions. After a year at the insurance company, Justin's work in local theaters opened another door for him—one that led him back to his original path. He left the corporate world to travel throughout the United States as part of a touring theater company.

The pieces of a career path puzzle may not come together for a while, but, as shown by the experiences of both Catherine and Justin, there is much you can do along the way to accumulate a lot of different puzzle pieces to maximize your chances of completing your own puzzle.

Starting Early

Building Your Skills

The workplace is in an almost constant state of change. Workers who succeed will be those who can be flexible, adapt to change, make decisions, and demonstrate initiative and the ability to learn. Good communication and teamwork skills are also important to develop.[1] The more well-rounded you can make your college experience, the better you position yourself as you enter the workforce.

For example, a knowledge of computer technology and the ability to use several word processing and database computer programs is a great asset. Different employers use different computer software programs. The more fluent you already are, the more attractive you will be to an employer looking for someone who doesn't first have to learn the computer language being spoken. Most colleges offer workshops in computer skills and courses in computer science. Take advantage of these opportunities. Not only will they help you in the job market, but they'll also help you with your work as a student. Courses and workshops on assertiveness, public speaking, and so forth can prepare you for your entry into the workforce. Make yourself as self-sufficient as possible. Word process your own papers in school, and do your own clerical work. This will give you another skill to present when you approach the job search.

While a 4.0 GPA won't necessarily get you jobs over someone with a 3.5, a low GPA could affect whether you're accepted to some corporate training programs. One graduate who had a low GPA discovered that it kept her from being accepted into some positions for which she was otherwise eligible. She decided to start temping first to establish her proficiency in the workplace. "After your first job," she says, "no one really asks about your GPA again." They do, however, for your first job, so approach your role as a student as practice for the real thing. Deal with your job as a student responsibly. Meet deadlines and follow through with all your commitments. Look at group projects as opportunities to learn what it means to be part of a team. Many employers look for evidence of this skill. Take an independent study course that demonstrates your initiative to develop a problem and a plan for researching and solving it.

As a club president, residence hall assistant (R.A.), student leader, varsity athlete, and so on, you can gain practical experience in what it means to work within an organization and the various power structures involved. As the social chair of your fraternity or sorority or as manager of an athletic team, you can develop valuable managerial and organizational skills. Work on the campus newspaper or assist with a monthly club newsletter to get practical publishing experience. Work in campus politics or as a volunteer in a community service agency to gain valuable experience in social issues and political change processes. Be able to recognize and communicate to an employer how these skills can transfer into that workplace.

The world is becoming more and more economically and politically interconnected, and the workforce is increasingly diversified. Successful workers will be those who can understand both men and women from a variety of cultures and backgrounds. In the year 2005, minorities and women together will make up the majority of the workforce.[2] By 2010, two-thirds of the new workers in the United States will be from groups currently labeled as minority groups.[3]

If you can understand and appreciate differences in people, you can incorporate these differences as a source of strength and creativity in any work environment.[4] Take advantage of opportunities while you're in college to learn about others and about yourself in relation to others. Enroll in multicultural and diversity education programs on campus, academic courses in ethnic studies, and activities that enable you to interact with people different from yourself. Challenge your assumptions and stereotypes about others. Allow yourself to work through, rather than back away from, the discomfort these challenges can provoke.

Practical Experiences and Internships

With accounting you take courses and learn from the book, but once you get out there it's a whole different ballgame.　—W.S.

Take advantage of opportunities to complement your academic program with practical experience. Part-time jobs provide some of those experiences. One graphic design major, for example, worked during college at a software company where she learned about desktop publishing and media design in a way she never learned in her classes. She encourages students to seek out experiences beyond the classroom and to explore many different jobs in the summers during college.

If you work during the summer, that doesn't mean you have to abandon the idea of enjoying your vacations from school. One graduate, for example, worked one summer as a counselor at a camp. She taught computer programming, which was related to her major, but she also got to be out in the country rather than in an office. She worked with kids in bathing suits rather than adults in three-piece suits, and she was able to windsurf during her free time.

Some colleges offer cooperative education programs in which students spend time out working throughout their academic programs. Others offer internships—an experience consistently mentioned by graduates as being the most valuable experience in their career development process. Those who didn't do internships said they wished they had. Consider internships early in your college career rather than necessarily waiting until your senior year. Look at internships as a chance to explore your dreams, not just the career path you're programmed on. This is the time to test out the possibilities—before you're committing to a job. This process will help you narrow your choices when the time comes to consider actual jobs. You can also learn a lot about what's important to you in the place you'll eventually work. Internships often lead to job offers with the employer after graduation. While you get to learn through the internship, the employer gets to test you out as a potential employee.

One graduate talks about how her full-time summer internship made her see what it was like to work from nine to five every day, dress appropriately, figure out transportation to and from work, and work while also living on her own in an apartment in a different city. She also learned a lot about what was expected from her as a professional.

> They were critical and very complimentary of my work, which is, I guess, the way it really is. And that was helpful. I guess I always wanted people to be sort of like a professor and always be giving me written and verbal feedback, but the nice thing was they gave me leeway, but they also gave me feedback, and it wasn't the same way a professor does. They treated me as an equal, and they expected things from me as an equal in terms of presentation and understanding the dynamics of being in the office. —C.T.

Early internship experiences can help you see gaps in your present skills and knowledge and perhaps guide some of your academic choices and work during the remainder of your college years. The skills and experience gained through internships are increasingly valued by employers. Some college career counselors are telling students to give as much attention to finding internships as they do to their grades.[5] The connections you make during your internships can lead to future job possibilities or, at the least, a valuable reference from someone actually working in the field.

Contacts and connections are an important resource, both

for information gathering and for getting your foot in some doors for interviews. One director of career development suggests starting to keep an address book from the day you enter college. Write down the name, phone number, and a word or two about anyone you meet who is interesting to you or remotely connected with your field of interest. Over the four years, this can give you a rich resource to consult in the future.

Chance connections are also helpful. Conversations on plane trips, waiting in line to buy movie tickets, or at the beach may reveal that the person you're talking to has the kind of job you're interested in. Or perhaps at a family Thanksgiving dinner you'll meet your cousin's new friend who happens to work for a company you want to know more about.

For some reason, undergraduates often express discomfort about spending time in the career development office. There is, however, no more valuable resource on your campus. Go in to the office early during your college career, and look around to find out what's available. If you go in *before* you're actually searching for a job, perhaps you'll feel less pressured. Sift through things. There may be files, bulletin boards, computer sources, and so forth. Talk to someone in the career development office about how its services work. Get to know a career counselor, and let her or him know what you're interested in. There will often be workshops offered and mailing lists you can get on to receive regular information.

Throughout your college years, be on the lookout for potential mentors—faculty members, staff members, job supervisors. A mentor is someone who has traveled across the bridge already and is able to support your journey. He or she is an adult who doesn't push those buttons your own parents sometimes do. "There's a big difference," one graduate says, "between commiserating about the job search process with your friends and talking it through with someone who is a few steps beyond where you are." This particular graduate found her mentor when she volunteered at a community service agency. Her mentor, the director of that agency, is the person who pushed her, and continues to push her, as a good coach pushes an athlete to perform up to her potential.

Self-Assessment

> All my life I've always wanted to be somebody. But I see now I should have been more specific.
> —Jane Wagner, *The Search for Signs of Intelligent Life in the Universe*[6]

The task of writing a résumé and planning a job search strategy can be overwhelming if you wait until the last minute. Keep an ongoing record of what you do—not just the jobs and activities, but also the specific skills you use and the leadership qualities you demonstrate. Over the course of your college years, you should be compiling a complete and varied list of what you can offer an employer. Identify where you may be lacking experience, and seek out opportunities to fill in the gaps.

A second self-assessment to undertake early in your college career is to figure out just what you enjoy doing—what makes you feel productive and successful, rather than what your parents want you to do, what you think you should do, or what will necessarily earn you the most money. We're talking about what you'll be spending thirty-five or more hours doing every week. Your career development office will have a variety of tests, tools, and programs to help you do some of this work. One approach is to focus initially not on particular jobs or careers, but on the kinds of factors that make you feel successful at a task.

Exercise: Success Analysis Chart

List below from five to ten achievements you have accomplished in your life so far. They don't have to be world-changing events; they need only to have felt like achievements to you (for example, got an A in organic chemistry, made the JV field hockey team, won second prize in the eighth grade talent show, R.A. in college, features editor of the college newspaper).[7]

1. _____

2. _____

3. _____

4. _____

5. _____

6. _____

7. _____

8. _____

_____

9. _____

_____

10. _____

_____

Now look over the lists below of what you may have put into and gotten out of these achievements.

What you put into this achievement:
   A. I used skill and know-how.
   B. I was free to decide what I did or how I did it.
   C. I influenced somebody and got the person to do what I wanted her or him to do.
   D. I helped someone else do something that was important to him or her.
   E. I met a challenge or took a risk.

What you got out of this achievement:
   F. I felt good about myself.
   G. I received recognition, support, or respect from others.
   H. I received money or some tangible reward.
   I. I received love and acceptance from my family.
   J. I learned something new.

Next to *each* of the achievements you listed, write the letters (A, B, etc.) to show *all* the things that describe why that item was an achievement to you. For example:

   1. Won second prize in eighth grade talent show—B, E, F, G, J
   2. R.A. in college—A, D, E, F, G, J

Now count up how many times each letter was written next to achievements.

A _____
B _____
C _____
D _____
E _____
F _____
G _____
H _____
I _____
J _____

To get your own personal definition of success, find the three letters written the most times. In the spaces below, write the three sentences belonging to them. This gives you your own personal definition of success.

I _____
and I _____
and I _____

By identifying what type of tasks or work make you feel successful and fulfilled, you can begin to explore career possibilities that will be more fulfilling for you. Talk to a career counselor. Will the careers you're interested in offer you the opportunity to feel successful according to your personal definition? If not, and if you still want to pursue that career direction, can you find other ways to have these needs fulfilled in your life?

Sift through career information you've been gathering. Narrow your focus. Some materials are best tossed out, others are best saved for the future. With the help of a career counselor, more actively pursue information about the particular types of jobs, geographical areas, and so forth that you're interested in. Begin to define specific job titles you want to pursue. Try to find a middle ground between being too vague (education) and overly specific (teach tenth grade history in my old high school). A middle-ground approach might be something like teaching at-risk adolescents.

Senior Year

> Maybe you legitimately want to do nothing but travel or work at alternatives for a year or two, but everyone should sit down with friends, a counselor, a professor, a parent, or somebody and figure out what you want to do next. You may have to bust your butt to network and do cover letters and résumés and test the waters to see what's out there. This is the best time to do it. I know I really have no idea what the hell I did with my time at college. But I'm sure I had three or four times as much leisure time as I do now and I did half as much as I do. Set aside one morning every week to do the job hunt. And if you have that introspective experience and decide that that's not what the next step is for you, that's fine. You don't want to be looking back and kicking yourself about all the free time you had. Going through my final semester in law school, I did this—what I didn't do in college.   —M.J.

Take M.J.'s advice and set aside time during your senior year to focus on the process. Some seniors approach the career and job search as they would a regular course in their schedule. If you haven't already become acquainted with the staff in the career development office on your campus, definitely get to know them during your senior year. They can guide, direct, and assist you as you make decisions about careers and jobs, develop a résumé, conduct a job search, and prepare for the interview process. Many career development offices also maintain files and information about alumni in specific fields, specialized placement services, and alternative programs such as public service, the military, and work abroad. Their libraries hold reference books such as *The Encyclopedia of Associations,* in which you can look up organizations appropriate to the careers you're considering. Calls to their national offices can bring in more information and additional sources to contact.[8]

If your career development office or campus computing center gives you access to the Internet, you can use various career oriented tools. Through the World Wide Web, for example, you can browse through different businesses and industries. You can also get information about careers and national organizations.

CareerMosaic (http://www.careermosaic.com/) is one service that lists information from various employers. Others include the National Association of Colleges and Employers' "Jobweb," (http://www.jobweb.org/), Online Career Center (http://www.occ.com/occ/), and Catapult (http://www.wm.edu/catapult/catapult.html). These kinds of networks can make much information available to you, but they're best used to gather information, not to actually apply for jobs. When you find jobs that you would like to apply for, use the more traditional cover letter and résumé approach to do so. One other caution: information on the Internet is unmonitored, which means that there's no guarantee that it's accurate or honest.

If job fairs, informational programs, and recruiting interviews are offered on campus or nearby, take advantage of them. Pick up material and keep it on file. Perhaps you and some friends can make a deal to go to different programs and pick up material to share with one another.

Once you identify professional organizations related to your chosen career field, join as a student member. The membership fees are lower for students, and you can often make contacts and get access to job listings.

Informational interviews, or talking with someone in a particular job about what they do, how they got there, and how they like it, are another good source of information. These interviews aren't designed to get you a job, but they can help you gather information and also make you visible to someone in the field. There's value in talking with both those who have been in a field for a while and those who are new to it.

If you're thinking about looking for a job overseas, start to conduct your job search from here. Talk to faculty and students who have been abroad about their experiences. If there are any companies nearby with overseas branches, talk to employees who have recently worked abroad. Don't plan to just sail off into the sunset; find out what job possibilities realistically exist for you first.[9] Refer to the section on traveling or working abroad later in this chapter for information on what to take care of before you leave.

As you seriously pursue the job search, keep track of what strategies work best for you. You'll most likely be searching again at various times in your life. It's becoming increasingly rare for someone to stay in only one job setting. The average person can expect to have at least six to eight jobs and to change fields three times during her or his working life.[10] Some of these changes will be voluntary as you decide to make a switch. Involuntary changes, however, are becoming more frequent. Organizational restructuring, downsizing of larger companies, increasing global competition, obsolescence of current industries, and growth of new ones as a result of expanding technologies all contribute to the fluid nature of today's job market. Develop your ability to deal with change, and look for how you can use your skills and talents creatively and in new ways.[11]

Develop your survival tools. Anticipate the kinds of situations that may shake your self-confidence, and decide how you will avoid letting that happen. The job search itself can certainly be one of those confidence shakers. One career counselor suggests reading your own résumé occasionally to remind yourself of who you are and what you do well. Or consider writing yourself a letter to be opened when you're feeling frustrated. Remind yourself, in the letter, of your strengths. A group of friends can also do this for one another. Put a support network in place now, so you can reach back to it if you need to. Perhaps your most accessible support will come from yourself—how you interpret and deal with your experiences. Your attitude can greatly affect how you approach things, and that in turn can affect how you come across to potential employers. Says one graduate, "turn 'this is scary' into 'this is exciting, and I can do anything.' "

Who Am I Anyway; Am I My Résumé?

At the start of the musical play *A Chorus Line,* one of the auditioning dancers plaintively asks that question. For the rest of the play, these Broadway hopefuls dance their hearts out trying to show who they are and what they have to offer. Throughout the audition, characters try to figure out what the director wants and how they can prove to him that they have it. Your written résumé needs to do the same thing as these dancers' physical résumé—present the right skills in the right language.[12]

Employers often skim through piles of résumés, so you need to stand out. This can happen both by what you say and by how you say it. Your cover letter should be no more than one page and should explain quickly how you learned of the job, what you have to offer, and how the employer can reach you. Find out who the appropriate person is to send the letter to, and address your letter to that person. Letters and résumés sent "To the Personnel Office" or "To Whom It May Concern" usually concern no one. Call the employer and ask to whom you should send your résumé. If you're told "the personnel office," ask for a name in the personnel office. Also ask for the correct spelling of the individual's name. Don't assume you know how to spell it. Be sure to type the envelope, even if you have to track down a typewriter to do so.[13]

There are many books on the market offering résumé

writing advice. Some computer software programs are also available. Career development offices have guidelines and will work with you as you develop your résumé. Take advantage of this guidance to help you craft the best possible résumé for your purposes. While your résumé should present you most favorably to potential employers, it should still be an honest representation of who you are. You may even find that you develop several different versions of your résumé to highlight different skills or experience, for different types of jobs, or to be faxed or computer scanned. As a college senior or a recent graduate, your résumé should be only one page long for an entry-level position. Some career counselors stretch this limit, and suggest that for some individuals, for some jobs, a résumé of up to, but no more than, two pages is acceptable. Your résumé should look balanced, be easy to read, and have lots of white space. Important information should stand out. Start your sentences with active verbs such as taught, developed, and created, and use vivid words whenever possible.[14]

Be specific about the skills you have that are most appropriate to this particular job. For some professions, portfolios, audition tapes, or other samples of your work should also be mentioned and made available upon request. Also feature your college degree early in the résumé. After several years of actually working, that work experience will become the focus of your résumé. For a new college graduate, however, the degree is your entrée to a career path.[15]

Consider these other informational categories for your résumé *if they show skills or experience related to the desired job*.[16]

Work experiences (both paid and nonpaid)
Relevant coursework
Research
Publications and presentations
Honors and awards
Activities and sports
Travel
Community service
Language and special skills

Employers often scan résumés looking for key words. The job ad or listing may include cues to some of those key words—skills or experience that they're looking for. If you have a chance to talk to people already working there, you will often hear some terms or ideas repeated. That can tell you about some of the employer's values and priorities.

There are three styles for presenting your résumé—chronological, functional, and a combination of the two. Functional résumés are most appropriate for entry-level jobs because the applicant generally hasn't yet built a chronological job record. The functional résumé focuses on skills rather than on the job in which they were learned.[17]

Researching Potential Employers

Do your homework before interviewing for any job. Learn as much as you can about the employer and the job you're applying for. Your career development office may have information on file or accessible through the Internet. If any alumni from your college work for this employer, ask about their experiences there. Read material (either in print or via

12. What is the goal of your work? _____

_____

Look back over your responses. Which of them are most crucial for you in any job you take?

_____

_____

_____

_____

_____

Interviews

A number of students begin job interviews during their senior year. Some of these take place on campus, when recruiters come to the career development office and interview potential job candidates. More frequently, however, employers do screening interviews over the telephone or have you come to their site for interviews if they're interested. A word of advice—you may get phone calls from prospective employers on your campus phone. Check the message on your phone answering machine. Replace the heavy metal rock background or the funny message that your friends thought was really cool. Go for a simple message that communicates to a potential employer that he or she has reached a serious candidate for a job.

Expect to have more than one interview before you're actually offered a position. You may also encounter some interviews where two, three, four, or more people will meet with you at once or one after the other. For this reason, always bring several extra copies of your résumé with you.

If and when you get an interview, be yourself. You may be

dressing differently than you do when you're in the residence hall or even going to class, but it's important that you still be yourself. If you pretend to be someone you're not, and you're hired, will that mean you have to pretend to be that someone else who interviewed every day that you go to work? One career counselor describes the job interview as "a kind of performance, but a performance of *you.*"

Besides doing your homework about the potential employer, get comfortable with yourself in an interview situation. Do practice interviews. Your career development office may offer interview workshops for this purpose, perhaps videotaping them so you can observe yourself. Ask friends to practice with you.

There are three general types of interview questions. The first type deals with your accomplishments—factual questions about your education, experience, and so forth. The second type is to help the interviewer get to know who you are and what you're all about. The third type is designed to help the interviewer look ahead and predict how well you might perform in the job.[20]

Factual questions are the easiest ones to respond to— "Have you done any traveling?" "What courses have you taken that relate to this position?" General open-ended questions about yourself can be harder to answer clearly and concisely—"So, tell me about yourself." Anticipate some of the kinds of questions you may be asked and think about how you might respond.

Don't focus on what a "right" answer is, but concentrate on what your honest answer would be. How you communicate in the interview is often as important as what you say.

Take your time responding. It's all right to take a moment to think about a question before talking. A response that sounds rehearsed and insincere won't help you as much as a thoughtful, honest, and personable interchange with the interviewer.

Questions go both ways. When you're asked if you have any questions, ask some good ones. Don't ask something that you should already know if you've done your homework in preparation for the interview. Interviews, as well as questions, work both ways. While the interviewer is trying to learn about and assess you, you should be evaluating the employer and the job. What is the actual job description? Where has this job led other people in the past? Who would you be working with? What kind of performance appraisal system do they use? Do you really want this job? Do you want to work with these people? Ask what you need to know to make a good decision if you're offered the position (except for salary; that should wait until you're offered the job).[21] If you ask similar questions at all your interviews, you can more easily compare various employers you see.

The Equal Employment Opportunity Commission (EEOC) has issued a guide to pre-employment questions that shouldn't be asked in job interviews or applications. You have the right to refuse to answer any questions that you feel could be used to discriminate against you in the hiring process. This includes questions about your marital status or plans to have children, your religious affiliation or holidays you observe, your age or date of birth (although they can ask if you're eighteen or of legal age for employment).[22]

Often inappropriate questions are asked by uninformed interviewers. Although you have the right to refuse to answer any improper questions, doing so can create some discomfort in the interview situation. One option is to avoid answering any inappropriate question that you think could hurt you. Some interviewers will back off in that event. If, however, there's a persistent pattern of insensitivity and improper questioning, you could point out diplomatically that you believe that question isn't really appropriate to ask or relevant to your ability to do the job. If you're not offered the job after being asked such questions, you *might* have grounds for a discrimination complaint if your refusal to answer those questions, or the answers you gave, led to your not being hired.[23]

You'll find it easier to relate to some interviewers than to others. While one person won't necessarily represent the entire staff, how you feel interacting with the interviewer could give you an indication of how you might feel or fit in at that company. On the other hand, if you don't click with the interviewer but do with others in the company, remember that the interviewer may have little direct contact with you once you're hired.

If they're interested in you, companies will want you to meet with a variety of people including the individual who would be your immediate supervisor. This is an important person to talk with. There are questions she or he can best answer since she or he is the person you'd be accountable to. Find out what you need to know. How is the flow of work structured, and what does the pace seem like? What are the expectations about work hours, weekend work, and evening work? Ask in a way that indicates that you're flexible because it may raise some eyebrows if the company style is that everyone works until things are done, regardless of the time involved. It's more appropriate to ask by saying that you want to be clear about what's expected so that you can be sure that you can meet those expectations and fulfill the commitment you make to the employer.

Meet a number of people in a variety of positions to get a better sense of how you would feel working there. If possible, spend part of a day in the workplace. This will help you see more clearly what the environment is really like there. You can also learn much from the interactions you see and hear as you wait for appointments. Remember, too, that they can gain impressions of you from your behavior as you wait. There may be informal opportunities for you to find out more about the workplace. Perhaps you can go to lunch with someone in the department or talk with staff who started out in the position you're interviewing for.

Don't discuss salary until you know that the employer wants to offer you the job. You're in your strongest negotiating position when they're eager to hire you.[24] Generally, if you're offered a job, there will be a salary range within which you can be hired. The offer within that range will be determined by your qualifications, background, and experience. Assess what you would bring to the position and ask for what you feel you're worth. Do some research beforehand about the market value of your degree and skills. Call the trade associations, employment agencies, and others in the field to gather information.[25] The National Association of Colleges and Employers (formerly the College Placement Council) publishes a salary survey. Check your career development office or the library for a copy.

Be prepared to back up your request based on your concrete qualifications and experience. As a college senior who will be starting your first job after graduation, you will probably find yourself entering near the lower end of a salary range. Experience gained through internships and summer work, and technological and computer skills, could increase your value to a potential employer. If you ask for more money than you're initially offered, and the offer remains firm, both you and the employer need to feel that you can accept the job and be content. Salary reviews and opportunities for advancement and increases as you gain experience can bring you up to a higher level within a specified period of time.

After you get home, reflect on your interview experience. What were your impressions of those you met? Were you treated as a person rather than as a product? How did you and your potential supervisor get along? Were people there overly obsessed with work? Did this feel like a place where you could be yourself and be relatively comfortable?[26]

Finally, remain open and flexible about your first job. Remember that your first job is just that, your *first* job. It won't be your last. It doesn't have to be perfect or your dream job. In fact, there's something to be said for starting out in your nondream job. We all make mistakes and learn as we go. Learning in a less than perfect job can give you some valuable tools and knowledge to put to use in that dream job that might be waiting across the next bridge. Sometimes a first job can get you in the door of a company even if you're not initially in the area you want to be in. Look at your first job as one in which you can learn and grow. You don't have to be there forever. Think of this as taking your first step rather than your final step. If you hold out for perfection, you may never move an inch.

> The most helpful advice that I got was to not be fixated on starting a career, to take the time and explore the possibilities, to not see myself as a failure if I wasn't instantly doing something fabulous after graduation. Think about your strengths and try to envision a wide range of possibilities rather than focusing on a single outcome. If you think that only one job is right for you, you might be setting yourself up for disappointment. Also, don't feel like a failure if your first job isn't up to your expectations— experiment and find out about what's out there. Change jobs and find a place where you will be happier.   —M.M.

Making the Transition

The transition to working life after college can be bridged in a variety of ways. One graduate, for example, developed an early internship into a part-time job during her senior year. That same part-time job continued after she graduated. During her senior year that job provided a balance in her life so she felt that she had a place in both the college world and the work world. She kept the job for a while after she graduated, and this gave her a familiar environment to work in while she considered her next move.

Still Looking?

Even if you actively pursue a job search throughout your senior year of college, you won't necessarily have a job by the time you graduate. Don't panic. Avoid setting rigid deadlines for yourself, or you might settle for *any* job just to have a job, and you could wind up unhappy or soon needing to job hunt all over again.

If you don't have a job when you graduate, keep looking. Often career development offices offer services to alumni, sometimes at no cost, sometimes for a small fee. As you continue your job search, keep your attitude positive. It can feel humiliating not to have a job, especially if you did really well in college. The job search, however, is a bigger ball game with many more players. Rejection letters are rejections of your qualifications as a candidate for a particular position, not of your qualifications as a candidate for all positions or of you as a person. Stay positive.

> I wish someone had told me how hard it was going to be making the transition from an environment where I was getting positive reinforcement about my intellect and abilities, to being an unknown. I think I started to undervalue my abilities and think "Oh my God, I can't really type and I don't know many kinds of software" instead of thinking, "I'm bright, well spoken, organized, intuitive, easily trained, creative, etc.; how can I put these talents to use?" I focused on what I couldn't do and felt unqualified for many positions, instead of looking at my strengths and trying to be creative about the possibilities.   —M.M.

One approach I used to take when I was rejected for a job I thought I was well qualified for, was to write a brief letter to the person who had interviewed me. I thanked him or her for considering me and said it would help me in the future if I could get some feedback about what specific skills or experience separated me out from those being considered further for the job. The feedback helped me see what areas I still needed to develop so I could either work to develop them or recognize that perhaps this job really wasn't the right one for me after all. I always felt stronger when I took the initiative to seek out this information. What I learned kept me from falling into a negative mind-set about my job search.

If you're continuing to search for a job after you graduate, stay connected to people who support you and make you feel good about yourself. It may be hard for you to be around friends who have jobs and talk about their work a lot. It may be hard for them not to talk about it. Agree on some middle ground you can both feel comfortable with.

Stay in touch also with your career development office and former professors. Go to local job fairs and meet people from the fields of interest to you. Many professional organizations have monthly meetings. This is also a way to make contacts. Let people—friends, relatives, acquaintances—know what kinds of work you're looking for and that you're available.

Get involved wherever you are. Get a part-time job or do volunteer work or play softball or sing in a community chorus. This can expand your circle of acquaintances, provide some fun and enjoyment, and let you get to know others in an informal setting. You never know when you'll discover, for example, that the person you've been sharing a recycling shift with all year happens to work at a company that might have some job openings that interest you.

Stay connected also to your college alumni association or those of sororities or fraternities, or other organizational networks from your school. Class notes in the alumni publications can keep you updated about where some folks are and what they're doing.

One graduate describes using her first five years out of college to do a lot of different things that helped to make her a more interesting person and also helped in her job searches. There are many ways to get where you want to go. A career counselor advises that you "look at it as a challenge—a learning situation. Have a good time doing it," she says. "Find the humor in it. Go for it in an organized way. Use the skills you've developed."

This includes using the job search strategies described earlier in this chapter. Continue to set specific goals for yourself even after you're no longer at school. While you may have long-term goals about where you would like to be in five or ten years, also set some reasonable short-term goals. Some of these might be in relation to your job search process.

- By February I'll have done three informational interviews.
- I'll talk with a career counselor back at school in October if I don't have a job by then.

Others may be in relation to what you want to accomplish in your first year after graduation.

- I will develop my computer skills during the first year out.
- I will work in an office regardless of the company and the specific job so I can learn as much as I can about how an office works.

Part-Time Work

If you don't have a full-time job yet, one option is to begin to work part-time. The positive side of this is that you can gain experience, develop your skills, and have at least some income while continuing to look for a full-time job. A part-time job might actually open the door to a full-time job by showing your strengths. If a full-time job opens up elsewhere in the company, you're already a known quantity. Part-time jobs can also let you feel more freedom than you would in a full-time job if a company expects many extra hours from full-time employees. The same problem, however, can arise with part-time jobs. Are you expected to put in the fifteen to twenty hours a week you're hired for, or is there an assumption that you'll work more than that if needed? If so, is there overtime pay, or are you expected to do it out of the goodness of your heart and personal work ethic?

Part-time jobs generally pay less than full-time jobs and don't come with the same fringe benefits. This means your health insurance would have to come out of your own pocket if you're not covered under your parents' policy.

If you're juggling more than one part-time job, you may wind up working more than full-time hours. Two halves often work out to be more than a whole in terms of total hours. It can also take extra emotional and intellectual energy. When I was holding two part-time jobs I found that it took an extra effort to fully shift my focus and attention when I traveled from one to the other.

Temporary Agencies

Temporary jobs are another option to explore if you're still looking for a job in your career path or if you haven't yet determined what direction you want to pursue. Temp work helps you pay the bills and also gives you the chance to try different kinds of jobs as well as different places of employment. Sometimes a foot in the door through a temp job done well in a large company will give you an advantage when a permanent job comes available. This is what happened to Justin, whose career path was described at the beginning of this chapter.

A job is work experience even if it's not directly in your field. Through temping you can accumulate work experience and develop skills that add to the scope of your résumé. You can also find out what it's like to work at a number of different places, and perhaps you can identify where you would like to work permanently someday. Temp work may pay less than a permanent job, but you can also continue to look and interview for a full-time permanent job. Temp salaries range from minimum wage to six dollars an hour for industrial jobs, to eight or nine dollars for clerical jobs, to higher for medical, legal, and technical jobs. Previous experience also helps increase your hourly wage.

If you're looking for temp work, you can locate temp agencies in the yellow pages under "Employment—Temp.", or some similar heading. The Sunday newspapers also carry ads from agencies. Pick an agency close to where you live. If you register with a national agency with branches throughout the United States, your information can be transferred to a different branch if you relocate. If you work for a temp agency during summers or vacations from college, you can build a good relationship that will help you get more responsible placements after you graduate. You can register with more than one temp service at a time, and you may want to shop around. Is the service an active and busy one? Do you feel comfortable with the person who interviews you? Some temp agencies offer benefits such as vacation and holiday pay after you've worked a certain number of hours for them.

Others offer bonuses and opportunities to purchase short-term medical insurance. Compare different agencies if these kinds of benefits are important to you.

When you go to register at a temp agency, approach it as you would a job interview. That's exactly what it is. Dress as you would for a job interview, and bring résumés and the names, addresses, and phone numbers of your references. There's generally a standard application to fill out, including information about your skills and previous employment history. You'll also need two forms of identification, one that documents your identity, such as a picture driver's license or ID or a voter registration card, and another that establishes your U.S. employment eligibility, such as your social security card or an original or certified birth certificate. Other acceptable documents include a U.S. passport, a naturalization certificate, or an unexpired foreign passport indicating unexpired employment authorization.

When you apply, the temp agency will evaluate your skills, educational background, and prior experience. If the agency decides to hire you, they will then send you out on temp jobs. Unless you severely limit your options by saying you'll only work at a small number of types of jobs or for a high hourly rate, you should be called within a week or two after you register. It shouldn't cost you anything to use a temp service. The employers pay the agency's fees. When the agency sends you out on a job, there's no additional interview. You go to work. You'll have a time card to be filled out by the job supervisor, and you return that to the temp agency, which then pays you.

The temp agency is your employer, and it's in your best interest to be a responsible employee. That means calling the agency immediately if you're sick and can't show up at a job you've been sent to, showing a professional and positive attitude, being on time, doing the work required, and working well with a minimum of supervision and without causing problems in the workplace. Companies may request you back if they're pleased with your work.

Temp jobs run for anywhere from one day to a week to longer, even several years. As a temp worker, you'll need to adjust to a new environment frequently. Dig in, ask questions, and get to work. Since it will be hard to develop friendships at work when you're changing work sites often, it's important to have friends, hobbies, or activities on the outside that fulfill these needs.

Starting a First Full-Time Job

SIBLING REVELRY   by Man Martin

Sibling Revelry, copyright © 1993 by Lew Little Ent. Reprinted with permission of Universal Press Syndicate. All rights reserved.

The adjustment to being part of the full-time workforce from being a student can be a big one. I was one of those students who worked hard all year and somehow managed to wait to get sick or fall apart from exhaustion until semester break. The working calendar doesn't have a semester break!

The rhythms of work are different from those of school and bring about positive changes too. You do more at work and less at home. Your free time becomes more free time. I remember picking up a mystery novel to read one weekend after I had graduated. I was enjoying it, but suddenly I noticed something strange. As I was reading, I'd been mentally underlining some of the text. Did I expect to be tested by some visiting detective about the details of the crime? I got over this old habit quickly.

> When I started work, I remember thinking that there would always be someone like a professor or advisor there to bail me out or hold my hand or tell me I was doing things right. —C.T.

The first day of work can bring some surprises. In college you're generally told what's expected of you. That doesn't always happen in real life. You won't necessarily get a syllabus to tell you what to do when. You may find yourself working independently and having to figure out for yourself how to organize your work and set and meet deadlines so it gets done. While you may have gotten a job description, and you may have talked about what you'd be doing, actually starting to do it can raise lots of questions. Ask them. Your supervisor may be more surprised if you don't ask any questions. Don't think that they expect you to know everything on the first day, or even the first week. You're not supposed to know everything. If you come across as if you do, that may raise more eyebrows.

Often you'll work as part of a team. Others will count on

you to be there and do your job. You can't cut work the way you might have slept through an 8:00 a.m. class in college. Share what you can, and be open to how others do things. You may discover areas in which you need more information or training. Take advantage of training opportunities offered, including seminars and workshops. Larger companies sometimes send employees to outside courses or programs. Workers willing to take risks by changing jobs within a company or taking on new assignments and succeeding do much to advance their careers.[27]

Observe the patterns of communication within the workplace. How formal or informal are they? Who gets called by their first names, and who doesn't? Does everything have to be put in a memo or sent by e-mail? Is there a hierarchy of who talks to whom and what channels have to be gone through? Who needs to give approval for something, who needs to just be kept informed, and who wants you to just do the job as you see fit?[28]

Learn also what is and isn't appropriate office behavior and what the informal structures and politics of the office are. Watch how others deal with situations. How do people handle disagreements? What's the appropriate way to ask for help, and whom do you ask first? What are the channels for resolving problems?

Get to know the unwritten office culture. Are you expected to, for example, make a fresh pot of coffee if you drink the last cup? Are activities like office parties or coffee breaks expected to be part of your plans even though that's not explicitly stated? Does passing up a break get interpreted as not being a team player rather than valued as indicating that you're a hard worker? Are you expected to give your life to the company, or are you expected to set limits and have a life outside?

Where I'm Coming From, copyright © 1993 by Barbara Brandon. Distributed by Universal Press Syndicate. Reprinted with permission. All rights reserved.

> I base most of my fashion taste on what doesn't itch.
> —Gilda Radner[29]

Casual dress in the business world is quite different from casual dress on campus. Find out what is and isn't appropriate in your new environment. For example, the computer firm where the Michael Douglas character worked in the movie *Disclosure* was pretty informal. At the start of the movie, much is made of the fact that he's wearing a tie that day only because he expects a major promotion. In other settings, the expectations are more formal. One graduate talks about how different it was to adapt to formal business dress when told that "women could definitely not wear pants—even tailored dress pants."

Build support and develop good working relationships to help you feel more a part of your new environment. Larger companies may offer groups for new professionals or activities like Friday afternoon bowling or aerobics classes. Ask the human resources office for information. Volunteer to serve on various committees and task forces as another way to get to know colleagues.

It will take some time to feel comfortable in your work environment. There may be a good number of recent graduates all starting together, and that can provide a natural social group. Often, however, you'll be the new kid on the block. Coworkers may be friendly, and some may reach out to make you feel welcome. However, it's not always possible to quickly form the type of intense relationships you had at college. Coworkers may have families and lives that are already quite full. Continue to get involved in activities outside of work to create a life for yourself.

One of the keys to succeeding in many work settings, especially in the corporate sector, is the ongoing support, sponsorship, and guidance of a mentor high up in the organization. This is important for anyone, but especially for those who have traditionally not had equal access to the powerful upper echelons of the business world. One important study attributes this type of help from above as a crucial factor distinguishing those women who had broken through the so-called glass ceiling—a transparent barrier that keeps women from rising above a certain level in corporations.[30] Cultural diversity programs should also go beyond recruitment efforts to mentor minority employees toward career tracks and access to all levels in a corporation.[31] Do you see any potential mentors for yourself in your job? Are they receptive to serving in this capacity? (The issues for today's employees of both genders and various cultural backgrounds are explored in a wonderful novel set in the banking world, *Brothers and Sisters,* by Bebe Moore Campbell.)

Taking Care of Yourself: Employee Rights

If you have reason to believe that your job may be in trouble, document any events that you feel are important. Keep copies of all your performance reviews and evaluations as well as any letters of recognition or thanks you receive.

You should similarly document any patterns of discrimination or harassment. Conflicts or grievances should be handled through your immediate supervisor and using the steps and channels in place to handle work grievances, including sexual harassment and discrimination complaints. Keep a log of the dates, times, locations, and people involved. Keep this log on file, and also tell someone else what's going on, even if you don't plan to pursue the issue at this time. If you choose to file a complaint, start within the channels of your organization. You can also file a Title VII complaint at a community equal employment opportunity agency or the state or regional office of the EEOC. If the management of a company is aware that harassment has been going on and they fail to deal with it, they can be held responsible.[32]

On the Road Again

> I had this idea that I had to get a job and be gainfully employed and make a living right away. I wish someone had told me you didn't have to do that. I had friends who knocked around and went through Europe or the United States instead of going right out and getting a job. If I had it to do over again, I would have traveled after graduation. Now I feel too old for that, too entrenched to be able to pick up and go.   —M.L.

You may decide to postpone your entry into the traditional workforce. The best time for doing something unorthodox or idealistic is generally during the first year or two after you graduate from college.[33] There are many options available that can contribute greatly to your personal growth and the development of skills that will benefit you throughout your life. These opportunities will expand your world. An alternate experience can also help you discover a new career path or look at your chosen direction in a new way.

Within the United States you can find a wide range of alternatives, many of which will provide room and board in exchange for service or work. Some examples, from the files of the Center for Interim Programs in Cambridge, Massachusetts, include:

- Internships teaching environmental education to groups of elementary through college-age students. Classes range from stream ecology to wild edible plants. The school has a plant study center, Appalachian archives, geology and fossil collections, and spinning and weaving workshops.

- Internships working with kindergarten through eighth-grade students at a Navajo boarding school. Work includes dorm duties, tutoring, coaching, library work, and so forth. Witnessing Navajo ceremonies and doing social service work in the community are also possibilities.
- Assisting at a family-centered primary health care program in rural Kentucky. Responsibilities include helping in a literacy and arts program in local public schools, taking medical supplies and mail to district clinics, and doing grounds and garden work.
- Internships at a wildlife sanctuary answering the wildlife rescue hotline, assisting with patient admissions, feeding animals and cleaning their cages, and helping in wildlife rescues or transports.
- Working at an educational and research oriented organization that cares for wolves in Colorado.[34]

Institutes, retreats, and other growth-type centers may also offer opportunities for you to learn and participate in their programs in exchange for doing needed work. Don't assume that there will always be formal programs advertised. Look for sites that interest you, then contact them and talk about what they need, what you can offer, and what mutual arrangements can be worked out.

There are a range of public service programs that allow you to do good and needed work, develop your skills and awareness, and receive some financial benefits. These programs will be hard work and will challenge you in many ways. VISTA, for example, is a full-time national service program that addresses the needs of low-income communities in the United States. Volunteers mobilize resources, recruit local volunteers, and help nonprofit community-based organizations build their services. VISTA volunteers serve a minimum of one and a maximum of two years. They receive either a stipend or an education award ($4,725 in 1994) at the end of each full year of service. The education award can be used to repay student loans or for additional educational training within seven years of the end of service.[35]

VISTA is now part of the AmeriCorps program sponsored by the Corporation for National and Community Service. Other AmeriCorps programs also involve young Americans, full or part time, to help communities deal with the challenges facing them in exchange for education awards to help pay back student loans or finance additional training in the future. The other national AmeriCorps program, in addition to VISTA, is the National Civilian Community Corps. Members live and train on downsizing military bases while participating in service projects in the surrounding area. Other AmeriCorps programs are based in local communities and involve work such as immunizing infants, tutoring teenagers, assisting victims of crime, reducing environmental risks, and working with the police and community members to preserve public safety. For information about all AmeriCorps programs, call 1-800-94-ACORPS or 1-800-833-3722 TDD.[36]

Teach for America is a national teacher corps that recruits recent college graduates who were not education majors to teach for two years in urban and rural public schools with limited resources. A summer preservice training program is provided, and Teach for America corps members then work as teachers in their own assigned classrooms, receiving ongoing support and feedback. They receive a first-year teacher's salary and also become involved in other school and community programs. For more information call 1-800-832-1230.[37]

The Peace Corps helps combat hunger, poverty, and lack of opportunity in less developed countries throughout the world. Peace Corps volunteers work closely with coworkers in host countries on projects that help people in those countries develop their resources to continue to make change themselves.[38]

Peace Corps volunteers serve two years (with the possibility of extending service) after three months of training. They receive a living allowance and have expenses covered. In addition, when volunteers return home after completing their commitment, they receive a readjustment allowance of $5,400. Some student loans may also be reduced, and many others are deferrable during the time of service.[39]

Acceptance into the Peace Corps requires that you have skills that are needed on the projects being staffed. Work in the Peace Corps can in turn develop additional skills and experience highly valued in the workplace and contribute to your competitiveness in the job market. The language, technical, and cross-cultural programs included in Peace Corps training are invaluable. There are also placement services available for returning Peace Corps volunteers. Call 1-800-424-8580 for Peace Corps information.[40]

Some graduates choose to explore the military as a post-college option. Graduates who have a military background—ROTC or the reserves—may qualify for officer candidate school. All others would enlist for a commitment of two to six years following a basic training period of approximately eight weeks. Enlistees can qualify for specific skills training in a wide variety of areas. Room, board, benefits, and a monthly paycheck are provided. There are also educational benefits, including a student loan repayment program and the opportunity to pursue an advanced degree with up to 75 percent of the expenses paid while remaining in the service full time. There are also many opportunities for travel and assignment abroad.

Military service is a far more structured environment than college or most any other situation you would choose. You're told what to do and how to do it, and there are no excuses. Should the United States become involved in any military operations, there is always the chance of being sent into action. A military commitment is not to be made lightly, so research this option seriously, including the differences among the various branches of the military (army, marine corps, navy, air force, coast guard), if you're considering this direction. Those who choose to make the military into a career will be eligible to retire after only twenty years. Many who do retire at that point collect their retirement benefits and are still free to pursue a civilian career once they're out. For more information about the military, look up the U.S. government recruiting stations in your telephone book.

Traveling or working abroad is an alternative that has proven invaluable to many graduates. Spending time in another part of the world can be especially beneficial in light of the expanding global economy. Experience abroad can increase your understanding of the world and give you a new perspective on your own culture.[41] You may head off on your own, through contacts made during your college years, with the advice of the career development or international study office, or through an organized program that places graduates in a variety of service or work situations.

Short-term employment abroad includes summer jobs; internships and training programs; work as an au pair, nanny, or mother's helper; farm work; and hotel or resort employment. Voluntary service positions can be found at work camps, archaeological digs and other field research projects, and cooperative projects that respond to human needs. Another type of work abroad is as a teacher of English in a variety of settings. Long-term employment overseas is difficult to secure because you need a work permit. Work permits will only be issued if the employer can convince her or his government that there is no local worker who can do the job she or he wants to hire you for.[42] Many organizations that sponsor students to work abroad charge a fee. Inquire about that before making any commitments.

The Council on International Educational Exchange, or CIEE (205 E. 42nd Street, New York, NY 10017; 212-661-1414), is a good initial contact for you to make. They publish, and update every two years, *Work, Study, Travel Abroad: The Whole World Handbook,* which describes more than twelve hundred programs. They will also send you, on request, a free copy of the latest edition of their *Student Travels* magazine. Copies are often available at college study abroad offices or international centers.

You'll need a passport to go to almost any foreign country and return. Apply in person at an authorized post office; a federal, state, or county courthouse; or at one of the thirteen national passport agencies several months before you plan to go. Bring with you proof of U.S. citizenship (a certified copy of your birth certificate or your naturalization certificate) and proof of identity, such as a valid driver's license. You'll also need two identical two-inch-square photographs. Ask at a photo shop for passport photos to be sure they meet all of the specifications.[43]

Some countries require a visa. This depends on where you're going, how long you plan to stay, and the purpose of your trip. Apply directly to the embassy or consulate (in the United States) of the country you want to go to. Get your visa before leaving the United States.[44]

CIEE sponsors an International Student Identity Card for travel-related discounts, accident and medical insurance, and access to a twenty-four-hour toll-free emergency hotline. A GO 25 International Youth Travel Card with similar provisions is available to anyone under the age of twenty-five. This would be the appropriate card for most college graduates to obtain.[45]

Some inoculations and immunizations are required for entry into specific countries, and others are recommended for your personal safety. Call the International Traveler's Hotline for current information (404-332-4559).[46]

Consular information sheets for specific countries provide information on health and safety conditions, unusual currency and entry regulations, and the locations of U.S. embassies and consulates. These can be requested from any of the field offices of the U.S. Department of Commerce, U.S. embassies and consulates abroad, any of the thirteen regional passport offices, and the Citizen's Emergency Center of the Bureau of Consular Affairs via touch-tone phone (202-647-5225).[47]

If you travel, be a responsible traveler and citizen of the world. Be socially and environmentally aware. Avoid doing things that damage the environment or disrupt the traditional way of life in whatever culture(s) you visit or work in.[48]

Increasing numbers of people with disabilities are traveling internationally and participating in international exchange programs. Mobility International is an organization working with persons with disabilities and the organizers of exchange programs to promote fuller involvement. The U.S. office of this group is located in Eugene, Oregon (503-343-1284). If you have a disability and want to pursue international opportunities, this organization is a good resource.[49]

Attitudes toward gay men and lesbians vary in different countries, cultures, and among different individuals. Travel guides in series such as *Let's Go* and the *Real Guides* include sections on issues for lesbians and gay men. Giovanni's Room (215-923-2960) and Renaissance House (212-674-0120), bookstores in New York, distribute a number of publications that give information on the social and political climate for gay men and lesbians in a variety of countries.[50]

A Few Last Words

The range of alternatives described in the last section have some advantages in common. They all provide an opportunity for you to break out of "business as usual" and perhaps take the road less traveled that poet Robert Frost described. As one alternative educator says, "Have your mid-life crisis while you're still young enough to enjoy it." [51]

You may not be able to, or want to, explore any of these alternatives right after college graduation. That doesn't mean they're lost to you forever. One of my colleagues, for example, spent time in the Peace Corps after many years of college teaching. If you pursue a career track immediately, consider using some vacation time to explore alternatives like those described. Maybe you can't make a one- or two-year commitment, but perhaps you can participate in month-long service programs or opportunities abroad. If your employer offers sabbatical time off or exchange programs, take advantage of those opportunities. You might even develop some of these if they're not already offered.

If you do something new and different, perhaps with people from a wide variety of backgrounds, you will gain wisdom, experience, and perspective that can come only from taking some risks and venturing off your current path. You may well return to that path—graduate school or a traditional career—a year or two down the road, but you'll be returning with far more than you left with. You will come back to your path with greater vision of where you want to go, a larger number of bridges into other areas to choose from, and a more powerful vehicle for making the trip.

> Exercise that talent which is your greatest gift, which you most delight to use, in the places or settings which appeal to you the most, and for the purposes most needed in the world.
>
> —Richard Bolles[52]

NOTES

Notes to the Introduction

1. August Wilson, *Fences* (New York: Plume, 1986), 97.

Notes to Chapter One

1. Nancy K. Schlossberg, *Overwhelmed: Coping with Life's Ups and Downs* (New York: Dell, 1989), 7.

2. Schlossberg, *Overwhelmed,* 27–29.

3. Daniel J. Levinson, with Charlotte N. Darrow, Edward B. Klein, Maria H. Levinson, and Braxton McKee, *The Seasons of a Man's Life* (New York: Ballantine, 1978), 51.

4. The idea for this exercise originated with the personal life map exercise described by George I. Brown in *Human Teaching for Human Learning: An Introduction to Confluent Education* (New York: Viking, 1971), 36.

5. Denise K. Magner, "Many Colleges Design Courses and Programs to Prepare Seniors to Live in the 'Real World'," *Chronicle of Higher Education,* March 21, 1990, A33.

6. Schlossberg, *Overwhelmed,* xvi.

7. Schlossberg, *Overwhelmed,* 38.

8. Morton A. Liberman, cited in Nancy K. Schlossberg, "A Model for Analyzing Human Adaptation to Transition," *Counseling Psychologist* 9, no. 2 (1981): 8.

9. Schlossberg, *Overwhelmed,* 48–53; Lawrence M. Brammer and

Philip J. Abrego, "Intervention Strategies for Coping with Transitions," *Counseling Psychologist* 9, no. 2 (1981): 27.

10. Schlossberg, *Overwhelmed,* 52.

11. George Caplan, cited in Schlossberg, *Overwhelmed,* 55.

12. Barrie Hopson, cited in Brammer and Abrego, "Intervention Strategies," 28.

Notes to Chapter Two

1. Ruth Klein, written communication to the author, 1968.

2. Wendy Wasserstein, "Uncommon Women and Others," in *The Heidi Chronicles and Other Plays* (San Diego: Harcourt Brace Jovanovich, 1990), 71.

Notes to Chapter Three

1. Beth Brophy, *Everything College Didn't Teach You about Money* (New York: St. Martin's, 1985), 156.

2. David W. Dunlap, "Rhode Island's Senate Sends Gay-Rights Bill to Governor," *New York Times,* May 20, 1995, 10.

3. U.S. Postal Service, *Mover's Guide,* Notice 8A, April 1989.

4. U.S. Postal Service, *Mover's Guide.*

5. Julia Gilden and Mark Friedman, *Woman to Woman: Entertaining and Enlightening Quotes by Women about Women* (New York: Laurel, 1994), 176.

6. David Savageau and Richard Boyer, *Places Rated Almanac: Your Guide to Finding the Best Places to Live in North America* (New York: Simon and Schuster, 1993), 25.

7. Savageau and Boyer, *Places Rated Almanac,* 126.

8. Maryland Department of Transportation Motor Vehicle Administration, *Welcome to Maryland,* V-272, August 1993.

9. Maryland Department of Transportation Motor Vehicle Administration, *The Guide for a Nonresident Permit,* VR-285, September 1992.

Notes to Chapter Four

1. Editors of Rodale Press, *Cut Your Bills in Half: Thousands of Tips to Save Thousands of Dollars* (Emmaus, Pa.: Rodale Press, 1989), 335–36.

2. Gloria Naylor, *The Women of Brewster Place* (New York: Penguin, 1982), 76.

3. Linda Bessette and Anne Owings Wilson, *From Paycheck to Power: The Working Woman's Guide to Reducing Debt, Building Assets, and Getting What You Want Out of Life* (Little Rock: August House, 1992), 44.

4. David Savageau and Richard Boyer, *Places Rated Almanac: Your Guide to Finding the Best Places to Live in North America* (New York: Simon and Schuster, 1993), 97.

5. Beth Brophy, *Everything College Didn't Teach You about Money* (New York: St. Martin's, 1985), 63.

6. Brophy, *Everything College Didn't Teach You,* 173–74.

7. Bessette and Wilson, *From Paycheck to Power,* 208–12.

8. Amy Tan, *The Joy Luck Club* (New York: Ivy Books, 1989), 161–81.

9. Bill Cosby, "Look Homeward, Sponger," in *Fatherhood* (New York: Berkley Books, 1986), 143.

10. Rodale Press, *Cut Your Bills in Half,* 13–15.

11. William Roberts, *How to Save Money on Just About Everything* (Laguna Beach, Calif.: Strebor Publications, 1991), 145.

12. Rodale Press, *Cut Your Bills in Half,* 6, 17.

13. Rodale Press, *Cut Your Bills in Half,* 8.

14. Rodale Press, *Cut Your Bills in Half,* 18.

15. Rodale Press, *Cut Your Bills in Half,* 6.

16. Ellen Goodman, "Eating Our Medicine," in *Value Judgments* (New York: Farrar, Straus, Giroux, 1993), 9.

17. University of California at Berkeley, *The Wellness Encyclopedia of Food and Nutrition: How to Buy, Store, and Prepare Every Variety of Fresh Food* (New York: Rebus, 1992), 26.

18. American Heart Association and Food and Drug Adminis-

tration, *How to Read the New Food Label,* Dallas, Tex., n.d. (brochure).

19. Jeff Smith, *The Frugal Gourmet Whole Family Cookbook: Recipes and Reflections for Contemporary Living* (New York: William Morrow, 1992), 43–54; *The Well-Equipped Kitchen* (Alexandria, Va.: Time-Life Books, 1978), 4–41.

20. Richard Nelson Bolles, *What Color Is Your Parachute? A Practical Manual for Job Hunters and Career Changers* (Berkeley, Calif.: Ten Speed Press, 1994), 419.

Notes to Chapter Five

1. David L. Scott, *The Guide to Personal Budgeting: How to Stretch Your Dollars through Wise Money Management* (Old Saybrook, Conn.: Globe Pequot Press, 1992), 90.

2. Scott, *Guide to Personal Budgeting,* 85.

3. Linda Bessette and Anne Owings Wilson, *From Paycheck to Power: The Working Woman's Guide to Reducing Debt, Building Assets, and Getting What You Want Out of Life* (Little Rock: August House, 1992), 46.

4. Bessette and Wilson, *From Paycheck to Power,* 44.

5. Beth Brophy, *Everything College Didn't Teach You about Money* (New York: St. Martin's, 1985), 13.

6. Brophy, *Everything College Didn't Teach You,* 14–15.

7. Bessette and Wilson, *From Paycheck to Power,* 57–63.

8. Brophy, *Everything College Didn't Teach You,* 10.

9. Brophy, *Everything College Didn't Teach You,* 13–14.

10. Brophy, *Everything College Didn't Teach You,* 10.

11. Editors of Rodale Press, *Cut Your Bills in Half: Thousands of Tips to Save Thousands of Dollars* (Emmaus, Pa.: Rodale Press, 1989), 154.

12. Rita Rudner, "If I Live in a Fantasy World, Why Do I Have to Pay Taxes?" in *Naked Beneath My Clothes: Tales of a Revealing Nature* (New York: Viking, 1992), 130.

13. Brophy, *Everything College Didn't Teach You,* 18.

14. Richard Nelson Bolles, *What Color Is Your Parachute? A Practical Manual for Job Hunters and Career Changers* (Berkeley, Calif.: Ten Speed Press, 1994), 345n.

15. Stuart Weinberg, certified public accountant, written communication to the author, July 21, 1995.

16. Weinberg, communication to the author.

17. Maxwell Associates, eds., *Reader's Digest Consumer Advisor: An Action Guide to Your Rights,* rev. ed. (Pleasantville, N.Y.: Reader's Digest, 1989), 178–79.

18. Brophy, *Everything College Didn't Teach You,* 64.

19. Maxwell Associates, *Reader's Digest Consumer Advisor,* 14–15.

20. Insurance Information Institute, *Nine Ways to Lower Your Auto Insurance Costs,* New York, n.d. (brochure); Nationwide Insurance Company, *Maryland Automobile Insurance Rating Information,* Columbus, Ohio, 1994 (brochure).

21. Federal Trade Commission, *Buying a Used Car,* Washington, D.C., March 1990 (brochure), 1.

22. Federal Trade Commission, *Buying a Used Car,* 1–3.

23. Federal Trade Commission, *Buying a Used Car,* 2, 4.

24. Federal Trade Commission, *Buying a Used Car,* 3.

25. Federal Trade Commission, *Buying a Used Car,* 5.

26. Maxwell Associates, *Reader's Digest Consumer Advisor,* 110–11.

27. James R. Ross, *How to Buy a Car* (New York: St. Martin's, 1988), 9–10.

28. Maxwell Associates, *Reader's Digest Consumer Advisor,* 116.

29. Maxwell Associates, *Reader's Digest Consumer Advisor,* 116.

30. Dave Barry, "Where You Can Stick the Sticker Price," in *Dave Barry Talks Back* (New York: Crown Publishers, 1991), 163.

31. Federal Trade Commission, *New Car Guide,* Washington, D.C., March 1992 (brochure), 1–2.

32. Federal Trade Commission, *New Car Guide,* 3.

33. Maxwell Associates, *Reader's Digest Consumer Advisor,* 118.

34. William Roberts, *How to Save Money on Just About Everything* (Laguna Beach, Calif.: Strebor Publications, 1991), 67–68.

35. Federal Trade Commission, *New Car Guide,* 4.

36. Maxwell Associates, *Reader's Digest Consumer Advisor,* 141–42.

37. Maxwell Associates, *Reader's Digest Consumer Advisor,* 138.

38. Maxwell Associates, *Reader's Digest Consumer Advisor,* 138.

39. Rodale Press, *Cut Your Bills in Half,* 61.

40. Maxwell Associates, *Reader's Digest Consumer Advisor,* 136–37.

41. Carolyn J. Rice, "How to Manage Money after Graduation," *Managing Your Career,* Spring 1991, 26.

42. Ruth Susswein, Bankcard Holders of America, quoted by Howard Henry Chen, "Had Fun with Your Credit Card? Now It's Time to Pay the Piper," *Baltimore Sun,* August 9, 1994, 1D.

43. Roberts, *How to Save Money,* 38.

44. Brophy, *Everything College Didn't Teach You,* 69.

45. Maxwell Associates, *Reader's Digest Consumer Advisor,* 181.

46. Bureau of Consumer Protection Office of Consumer and Business Education, *Facts for Consumers: Choosing and Using Credit Cards,* Federal Trade Commission, Washington, D.C., February 1993 (brochure), 1–6.

47. Board of Governors of the Federal Reserve System, *Consumer Handbook to Credit Protection Laws* (Washington, D.C.; Board of Governors of the Federal Reserve System, 1993), 17–19; Bureau of Consumer Protection, *Choosing and Using Credit Cards*; Barnes and Noble Bookstores, Inc., *Credit: Why to Get It. When to Use It. How to Keep It,* 1992 (brochure).

48. Bureau of Consumer Protection Office of Consumer and Business Education, *Facts for Consumers: Solving Credit Problems,* Federal Trade Commission, Washington, D.C., May 1992 (brochure), 7.

49. Niki Scott, "College Loan May Turn into a Future Financial Burden," *Baltimore Sun,* July 3, 1994, 4J.

50. Rice, "How to Manage Money," 16.

51. Board of Governors of the Federal Reserve System, *Making*

Sense of Savings (Washington, D.C.; Board of Governors of the Federal Reserve System, n.d.), 1.

52. Federal Reserve System, *Making Sense*, 2.

53. Federal Reserve System, *Making Sense*, 5.

54. Federal Reserve System, *Making Sense*, 3.

55. Federal Reserve System, *Making Sense*, 3.

56. Federal Reserve System, *Making Sense*, 4.

57. Federal Reserve System, *Making Sense*, 5.

58. Maxwell Associates, *Reader's Digest Consumer Advisor*, 221.

59. Federal Reserve System, *Making Sense*, 6–9.

60. Career Opportunity News, *Fringe Benefits: The Other Side of the Paycheck*, Garrett Park, Md., n.d. (handout).

61. Rodale Press, *Cut Your Bills in Half*, 350.

62. Financial Literacy Center, *11 Ways to Make the Most of Your 401(k)*, Kalamazoo, Mich., n.d. (brochure).

63. Quotesmith Corporation, "News Flash!" Darien, Ill., 1995 (news release).

64. Rudner, "Rethinking Chapter 31," in *Naked Beneath My Clothes*, 137.

65. Roberts, *How to Save Money*, 46.

66. Insurance Information Institute, *Nine Ways to Lower Your Auto Insurance Costs*; Nationwide Insurance Company, *Maryland Automobile Insurance Rating Information*.

67. Roberts, *How to Save Money*, 51.

68. Brophy, *Everything College Didn't Teach You*, 52; Maxwell Associates, *Reader's Digest Consumer Advisor*, 251.

69. Brophy, *Everything College Didn't Teach You*, 51.

70. Benji O. Anosike, *How to Plan Your "Total" Estate with a Will and Living Will without Lawyer's Fees* (Newark, N.J.: Do-It-Yourself Legal Publishers, 1995), 7–8.

Notes to Chapter Six

1. "After College, a Search for a Job and for Health Coverage," *New York Times*, May 31, 1994, A12.

2. Patricia Meisol, "Uninsured Grads Feel Invincible, but Take Big Risk," *Baltimore Evening Sun,* May 23, 1995, 1D, 5D.

3. "After College," A12.

4. Art Ulene and Val Ulene, *How to Cut Your Medical Bills* (Berkeley, Calif.: Ulysses Press, 1994), 23.

5. Ulene and Ulene, *Cut Your Medical Bills,* 24.

6. Quotesmith Corporation, "News Flash!" Darien, Ill., 1995 (news release).

7. Ulene and Ulene, *Cut Your Medical Bills,* 21.

8. Ulene and Ulene, *Cut Your Medical Bills,* 11.

9. Ulene and Ulene, *Cut Your Medical Bills,* 25.

10. Ulene and Ulene, *Cut Your Medical Bills,* 23.

11. Ulene and Ulene, *Cut Your Medical Bills,* 30.

12. Editors of Rodale Press, *Cut Your Bills in Half: Thousands of Tips to Save Thousands of Dollars* (Emmaus, Pa.: Rodale Press, 1989), 363.

13. Ulene and Ulene, *Cut Your Medical Bills,* 15–17.

14. David R. Stutz, Bernard Feder, and the Editors of Consumer Reports Books, *The Savvy Patient: How to Be an Active Participant in Your Health Care* (Mount Vernon, N.Y.; Consumers Union, 1990), 113.

15. Ulene and Ulene, *Cut Your Medical Bills,* 45.

16. Ulene and Ulene, *Cut Your Medical Bills,* 34.

17. Maxwell Associates, eds., *Reader's Digest Consumer Advisor: An Action Guide to Your Rights,* rev. ed. (Pleasantville, N.Y.: Reader's Digest, 1989), 296–97.

18. David Savageau and Richard Boyer, *Places Rated Almanac: Your Guide to Finding the Best Places to Live in North America* (New York: Simon and Schuster, 1993), 210.

19. Stutz, Feder, et al., *The Savvy Patient,* 16.

20. Stutz, Feder, et al., *The Savvy Patient,* 101.

21. Stutz, Feder, et al., *The Savvy Patient,* 77–82.

22. Ulene and Ulene, *Cut Your Medical Bills,* 80; Stutz, Feder, et al., *The Savvy Patient,* 107.

23. Ulene and Ulene, *Cut Your Medical Bills,* 80; Stutz, Feder, et al., *The Savvy Patient,* 107.

24. Ulene and Ulene, *Cut Your Medical Bills,* 80; Stutz, Feder, et al., *The Savvy Patient,* 107.

25. Ulene and Ulene, *Cut Your Medical Bills,* 75.

26. Ulene and Ulene, *Cut Your Medical Bills,* 55–56, 63.

27. Ulene and Ulene, *Cut Your Medical Bills,* 64–67.

28. Stutz, Feder, et al., *The Savvy Patient,* 130.

29. Stutz, Feder, et al., *The Savvy Patient,* 117–18.

30. Stutz, Feder, et al., *The Savvy Patient,* 238–39.

31. Stutz, Feder, et al., *The Savvy Patient,* 232–37.

32. Department of Health and Human Services, *Safe and Sure Self-Care with Over-the-Counter Medicines,* Food and Drug Administration, Rockville, Md., 1992 (brochure).

33. Lawrence Galton, *1001 Health Tips* (New York: Simon and Schuster, 1984), 165–66.

34. Judith Levine Willis, *Using Over-the-Counter Medications Wisely,* Food and Drug Administration, Rockville, Md., 1992 (brochure).

35. Maxwell Associates, *Reader's Digest Consumer Advisor,* 297.

36. Ulene and Ulene, *Cut Your Medical Bills,* 208–16.

37. Dave Barry, "Dentistry Self-Drilled," in *Dave Barry's Bad Habits* (New York: Holt, 1987), 157–58.

38. Ulene and Ulene, *Cut Your Medical Bills,* 140–41.

39. Ulene and Ulene, *Cut Your Medical Bills,* 175–82.

Notes to Chapter Seven

1. Scott H. Plantz with Nicholas Y. Lorenzo and Jesse A. Cole, *Getting into Medical School: Strategies for the 90's* (New York: Prentice Hall, 1990), 18–19.

2. Plantz et al., *Getting into Medical School,* 50.

3. *MBA Q and A* (Santa Monica, Calif.; Graduate Management Admission Council, 1994), 14.

4. Plantz et al., *Getting into Medical School,* 79.

5. Plantz et al., *Getting into Medical School,* 60–75.

6. Plantz et al., *Getting into Medical School,* 92.

7. *Graduate School Guide,* 25th ed. (New Rochelle, N.Y.: School Guide Publications, 1995), 6.

8. *Graduate School Guide,* 5.

9. *MBA Q and A,* 24.

10. *Graduate School Guide,* 6.

11. *Graduate School Guide,* 6.

12. American Academy of Physician Assistants, *Information on the Physician Assistant Profession,* Alexandria, Va., 1994 (brochure).

Notes to Chapter Eight

1. Shena Crane, "Today's Evolving Workplace," *Employment Outlook in The Baltimore Sun,* September 28, 1994, 9.

2. Steven D. Kaye, cited in Shena Crane, *What Do I Do Now? Making Sense of Today's Changing Workplace* (Irvine, Calif.: Vista Press, 1994), 154.

3. Thomas G. Exter, cited in Crane, *What Do I Do Now?* 154.

4. Catherine S. Buntaine and Martha N. Johnson, "16 Commonly Asked (and Unasked) Questions about Cultural Diversity and Organizations" (Cincinnati: Caleel Jamison Consulting Group, 1991), 1.

5. Ben Gose, "More Jobs?" *Chronicle of Higher Education,* May 18, 1994, A28.

6. Jane Wagner, *The Search for Signs of Intelligent Life in the Universe* (New York: HarperPerennial, 1990), 35.

7. Adapted from an exercise distributed by Dr. Joel Goodman, president of the Humor Project, Saratoga Springs, New York, in a course at the University of Massachusetts, Amherst, 1974.

8. Donald Asher, *From College to Career: Entry-Level Résumés for Any Major* (Berkeley, Calif.: Ten Speed Press, 1992), 14.

9. Richard Nelson Bolles, *What Color Is Your Parachute? A Practical Manual for Job Hunters and Career Changers* (Berkeley, Calif.: Ten Speed Press, 1994), 143.

10. Bolles, *What Color Is Your Parachute?* 15.

11. Crane, *What Do I Do Now?* 7–16.

12. Asher, *From College to Career,* 16.

13. Martin John Yate, *Résumés That Knock 'Em Dead* (Holbrook, Mass.: Bob Adams, 1993), 54; Ron Fry, *Your First Interview: Everything You Need to Know to "Ace" the Interview and Get Your First Job* (Hawthorne, N.J.: Career Press, 1991), 22–24.

14. Asher, *From College to Career,* 28–29, 67.

15. Asher, *From College to Career,* 39, 43.

16. Asher, *From College to Career,* 18.

17. Yate, *Résumés,* 9–10.

18. Asher, *From College to Career,* 165; Fry, *Your First Interview,* 12–16.

19. Some of the ideas in this exercise were adapted from Neil Yeager, *Career Map: Deciding What You Want, Getting It, and Keeping It!* (New York: Wiley, 1988), 41–47, 246–50.

20. Fry, *Your First Interview,* 103.

21. Fry, *Your First Interview,* 115–19.

22. Fry, *Your First Interview,* 124–25.

23. Fry, *Your First Interview,* 126–29.

24. Beth Brophy, *Everything College Didn't Teach You about Money* (New York: St. Martin's, 1985), 148–49.

25. Brophy, *Everything College Didn't Teach You,* 148.

26. Fry, *Your First Interview,* 139–41.

27. Ann M. Morrison, Randall P. White, Ellen Van Velsor, and the Center for Creative Leadership, *Breaking the Glass Ceiling: Can Women Reach the Top of America's Largest Corporations?* updated ed. (Reading, Mass.: Addison-Wesley, 1992), 57–60.

28. Yeager, *Career Map,* 246.

29. Julia Gilden and Mark Friedman, *Woman to Woman: Entertaining and Enlightening Quotes by Women about Women* (New York: Laurel, 1994), 137.

30. Morrison, et al., *Breaking the Glass Ceiling,* 13, 25.

31. Crane, *What Do I Do Now?* 155–56.

32. Dan Lacey with the editors of Nolo Press, *Your Rights in*

the Workplace (Berkeley, Calif.: Nolo Press, 1991), 3/5, 5/6, 5/7, 6/7.

33. Asher, *From College to Career,* 43.

34. Cornelius Bull, *The Center for Interim Programs* (Cambridge, Mass.; Center for Interim Programs, n.d.), 7–12.

35. "AmeriCorps Extends VISTA's Tradition of Service," *National VISTA News,* Winter 1994, 1, 6.

36. *Learn and Serve America: Higher Education Application Guidelines* (Washington, D.C.; Corporation for National Service, 1995), 63–64.

37. *Teach for America Application 1995* (New York; Teach for America, 1994).

38. *Peace Corps: The Toughest Job You'll Ever Love* (Washington, D.C.; Peace Corps, 1993), 2–4.

39. *Peace Corps,* 5, 10.

40. Peace Corps, *African Americans in the Peace Corps of the United States of America,* Washington, D.C., 1991 (brochure).

41. Lázaro Hernández and Max Terry, eds., *Work, Study, Travel Abroad: The Whole World Handbook,* 12th ed. (New York: St. Martin's, 1994), 1.

42. Hernández and Terry, *Work, Study, Travel Abroad,* 17–29.

43. Hernández and Terry, *Work, Study, Travel Abroad,* 4.

44. Hernández and Terry, *Work, Study, Travel Abroad,* 5.

45. Hernández and Terry, *Work, Study, Travel Abroad,* x–xi.

46. Hernández and Terry, *Work, Study, Travel Abroad,* 6.

47. Hernández and Terry, *Work, Study, Travel Abroad,* 8–9.

48. Hernández and Terry, *Work, Study, Travel Abroad,* 2–3.

49. Hernández and Terry, *Work, Study, Travel Abroad,* 13.

50. Hernández and Terry, *Work, Study, Travel Abroad,* 14.

51. Cornelius Bull, personal communication to the author, June 28, 1995.

52. Richard Bolles, cited in "Career as an Imaginative Quest," by Garrett McAuliffe, *American Counselor* 2, no. 1 (1993): 16.

ADDITIONAL RESOURCES

Books

Applegarth, Ginger. *The Money Diet: Reaping the Rewards of Financial Fitness.* New York: Penguin, 1995.

Asher, Donald. *From College to Career: Entry-Level Résumés for Any Major.* Berkeley, Calif.: Ten Speed Press, 1992.

Benjamin, Medea, and Andrea Freedman. *Bridging the Global Gap: A Handbook to Linking Citizens of the First and Third Worlds.* Cabin John, Md.: Seven Licks Press, 1989.

Benson, John. *Transformative Adventures, Vacations, and Retreats: An International Directory of 300 Plus Host Organizations.* Portland, Oreg.: New Millennium, 1994.

Bessette, Linda, and Anne Owings Wilson. *From Paycheck to Power: The Working Woman's Guide to Reducing Debt, Building Assets, and Getting What You Want Out of Life.* Little Rock: August House, 1992.

Bolles, Richard Nelson. *What Color Is Your Parachute? A Practical Manual for Job Hunters and Career Changers.* Berkeley, Calif.: Ten Speed Press, revised each year.

Bridges, William. *Transitions: Making Sense of Life's Changes.* Reading, Mass.: Addison-Wesley, 1980.

———. *Transitions: Making the Most of Change.* Reading, Mass.: Addison-Wesley, 1991.

Brophy, Beth. *Everything College Didn't Teach You about Money.* New York: St. Martin's, 1985.

Carter, Carol, and Gary June. *Graduating into the Nineties: Getting the Most Out of Your First Job after College.* New York: Farrar, Straus, Giroux, 1993.

Cassidy, Daniel J. *The Graduate Scholarship Book.* 2d ed. New York: Prentice Hall, 1990.

Christiano, Richard, ed. *Volunteer! The Comprehensive Guide to Voluntary Service in the U.S. and Abroad.* 5th ed. New York: Council on International and Educational Exchange, 1995.

Consumer Reports Books Editors. *Complete Drug Reference, 1994: United States Pharmacopeia.* Yonkers, N.Y.: Consumer Reports Books, 1993.

Crane, Shena. *What Do I Do Now? Making Sense of Today's Changing Workplace.* Irvine, Calif.: Vista Press, 1994.

Everett, Carole Bober, and Tracy Cummings Harkins. *The After-College Guide to Life.* Severna Park, Md.: Alcove Press, 1993.

Ewing, David W. *Inside Harvard Business School: Strategies and Lessons of America's Leading School of Business.* New York: Random House, 1990.

Feingold, Norman S., and Marilyn N. Feingold. *The Complete Job and Career Handbook: 101 Ways to Get from Here to There.* Garrett Park, Md.: Garrett Park Press, 1993.

Feingold, Norman S., and Glenda A. Hansard-Winkler. *A Comprehensive Directory of 1200 Journals Listing Career Opportunities.* Garrett Park, Md.: Garrett Park Press, 1989.

Fox, Paul G. *Thriving in Tough Times.* Hawthorne, N.J.: Career Press, 1992.

Gomez-Preston, Cheryl, with Randi Reisfeld. *When No Means No: A Guide to Sexual Harassment.* New York: Birch Lane, 1993.

Harragan, Betty Lehan. *Games Mother Never Taught You: Corporate Gamesmanship for Women.* Rev. ed. New York: Warner Books, 1989.

Hartel, William, Stephen Schwartz, Steven Blume, and John N. Gardner. *Ready for the Real World.* Belmont, Calif.: Wadsworth, 1994.

Healy, Lisa, ed. *My First Year in Book Publishing: Real World Stories from America's Book Publishing Professionals.* New York: Walker, 1994.

Hernández, Lázaro, and Max Terry, eds. *Work, Study, Travel Abroad: The Whole World Handbook*. 12th ed. New York: St. Martin's, 1994 (updated every two years).

J. K. Lasser's Your Income Tax. New York: Macmillan, 1994 (updated every year).

Kane, Pearl Rock, ed. *The First Year of Teaching: Real World Stories from America's Teachers*. New York: Mentor, 1991.

Kastre, Michael F., Nydia Kastre, and Alfred G. Edwards. *The Minority Career Guide—What African Americans, Hispanics, and Asian Americans Must Know to Succeed in Corporate America*. Princeton, N.J.: Peterson's, 1993.

Keeslar, Oreon, and Judy K. Santamaria. *Financial Aids for Higher Education*. 16th ed. Madison, Wis.: Brown and Benchmark, 1995.

Keirsey, David, and Marilyn Bates. *Please Understand Me: Character and Temperament Types*. 3d ed. Del Mar, Calif.: Prometheus Nemesis, 1978.

Klass, Perri. *A Not Entirely Benign Procedure: Four Years as a Medical Student*. New York: NAL Dutton, 1994.

Langelan, Martha J. *Back Off! How to Confront and Stop Sexual Harassment and Harassers*. New York: Fireside, 1993.

Langone, John. *Harvard Med: The Story behind America's Premier Medical School and the Making of America's Doctors*. New York: Crown, 1995.

Lathrop, Richard. *Who's Hiring Who?* Rev. ed. Berkeley, Calif.: Ten Speed Press, 1994.

Leape, Martha P., and Susan Vacca. *The Harvard Guide to Careers*. 3d ed. Cambridge, Mass.: Harvard University Press, 1991.

Levinson, Daniel J., with Charlotte N. Darrow, Edward B. Klein, Maria H. Levinson, and Braxton McKee. *The Seasons of a Man's Life*. New York: Ballantine, 1978.

Lowell, James. *How to Survive in the Real World: Financial Independence for the Recent Graduate*. New York: Penguin, 1995.

McCarthy, Claire. *Learning How the Heart Beats: The Making of a Pediatrician*. New York: Viking Penguin, 1995.

McMillon, Bill. *Volunteer Vacations: Short-Term Adventures that Will*

Benefit You and Others. 4th ed. Chicago: Chicago Review Press, 1993.

Morris, Celia. *Bearing Witness: Sexual Harassment and Beyond—Everywoman's Story*. Boston: Little, Brown, 1994.

Morrison, Ann M., Randall P. White, Ellen Van Velsor, and the Center for Creative Leadership. *Breaking the Glass Ceiling: Can Women Reach the Top of America's Largest Corporations?* 2d ed. Reading, Mass.: Addison-Wesley, 1992.

Plantz, Scott H., with Nicholas Y. Lorenzo, and Jesse A. Cole. *Getting into Medical School: Strategies for the 90's*. 2d ed. New York: Prentice Hall, 1993.

Ramsdell, Melissa, ed. *My First Year as a Doctor: Real World Stories from America's M.D.s*. New York: Walker, 1994.

Raymond, Alan G. *The HMO Health Care Companion*. New York: HarperPerennial, 1994.

Reinhold, Barbara. *Toxic Work: Overcoming Stress, Burn-Out, and Overload and Revitalizing Your Career*. New York: E. P. Dutton, 1996.

Repa, Barbara K., with the Editors of Nolo Press. *Your Rights in the Workplace*. 2d ed. Berkeley, Calif.: Nolo Press, 1993.

Roberts, William. *How to Save Money on Just About Everything*. Laguna Beach, Calif.: Strebor Publications, 1991.

Robinson, Peter. *Snapshots from Hell: The Making of an MBA*. New York: Warner Books, 1994.

Editors of Rodale Press. *Cut Your Bills in Half: Thousands of Tips to Save Thousands of Dollars*. New York: Smithmark, 1993.

Rogers, Adam. *The Intrepid Traveler: Getting the Ultimate Experience for Your Travel Dollars*. 2d ed. Los Angeles: Global View Press, 1993.

Ross, James R. *How to Buy a Car*. 3d ed. New York: St. Martin's, 1993.

Sachs, Leslie R. *How to Buy Your New Car for a Rock Bottom Price*. New York: NAL Dutton, 1987.

Savageau, David, and Richard Boyer. *Places Rated Almanac: Your Guide to Finding the Best Places to Live in North America*. New York: Simon and Schuster, 1993.

Schlachter, Gail Ann, and R. David Weber. *Directory of Financial Aids for Minorities.* 5th ed. San Carlos, Calif.: Reference Service Press, 1993.

Schlossberg, Nancy K. *Overwhelmed: Coping with Life's Ups and Downs.* New York: Dell, 1989.

Simenhoff, Mark, ed. *My First Year as a Lawyer: Real World Stories from America's Lawyers.* New York: Walker, 1994.

Steingold, Fred S. *The Employer's Legal Handbook.* Berkeley, Calif.: Nolo Press, 1994.

Sumrall, Amber Coverdale, and Dena Taylor. *Sexual Harassment: Women Speak Out.* Freedom, Calif.: Crossing Press, 1992.

Tener, Elizabeth. *The Smith College Job Guide: How to Find and Manage Your First Job.* New York: NAL Dutton, 1991.

Thomas, G. Scott. *The Rating Guide to Life in America's Small Cities.* Buffalo, N.Y.: Prometheus Books, 1990.

Turow, Scott. *One L: The Turbulent Story of a First Year at Harvard Law School.* New York: Warner Books, 1988.

Ulene, Art, and Val Ulene. *How to Cut Your Medical Bills.* Berkeley, Calif.: Ulysses Press, 1994.

Vickery, Donald M., and James F. Fries. *Take Care of Yourself: Your Personal Guide to Self-Care and Preventing Illness.* 5th ed. Reading, Mass.: Addison-Wesley, 1993.

Witt, Melanie Astaire. *Job Strategies for People with Disabilities: Enable Yourself for Today's Job Market.* Princeton, N.J.: Peterson's, 1992.

Yeager, Neil. *Career Map: Deciding What You Want, Getting It, and Keeping It!* New York: Wiley, 1988.

Other Publications

Bottom Line Personal
P.O. Box 58446
Boulder, CO 80322
The purpose of this twice-monthly publication is to give people who are busy with their careers information to help them handle their personal lives more effectively. Information and tips are provided by

knowledgeable sources in areas such as automobiles, banking, careers, health, credit management, families, financial planning, homes, insurance, interest rates, investments, estate planning, law, money management, psychology, real estate, security, sexuality, taxes, time management, travel, and forecasting trends.

Consumer Information Catalog

Consumer Information Center, 4C

P.O. Box 100 Pueblo, CO 81002

This regularly published catalog describes free and low-cost federal publications of consumer interest. You can order directly. Areas of information include cars, food and nutrition, health, housing, finances, employment, federal programs, and benefits.

Consumer Reports

Consumers Union of United States, Inc.

101 Truman Avenue

Yonkers, NY 10703-1057

This is a monthly publication by Consumers Union, an independent, nonprofit testing and information center serving consumers. The Union is a comprehensive source of unbiased advice about products and services, personal finance, health, nutrition, and other consumer issues. They buy and test products, survey readers, and report on the results. Monthly newsletters on travel and health are also published. Information is available electronically via America Online, CompuServe, Knight-Ridder, Nexis, and Prodigy and on CD-ROM. Contact the Consumer Union Electronic Publishing Department at the address above.

Transitions Abroad

For free sample copy:

18 Hulst Road

P.O. Box 344

Amherst, MA 01004

For subscription:

Department TRA

P.O. Box 3000

Denville, NJ 07834

This is a bimonthly magazine focusing on economy travel, overseas study programs, work opportunities, and educational travel. It offers practical information plus firsthand reports from travelers. An annual review is published in the July-August issue.

Videos, TV Shows, Plays

The Big Chill. A group of college friends revive the ties that bind them during the course of a weekend. Video.

A Chorus Line. Broadway dancers experience the job interview of a lifetime. Musical play and video.

Ellen. A group of friends live and work in L.A. TV series.

ER. A medical student is one of the main characters in this slice-of-life hospital show. TV series.

Everybody's All American. A football hero has trouble leaving his glory days behind and moving on, while his college sweetheart–wife changes and grows. From the novel by Frank Deford. Video.

Friends. A group of friends live in New York and deal with many of the issues faced by twentysomethings. TV series.

Gross Anatomy. First-year medical students negotiate the challenges of the task ahead. Video.

Living Single. A group of young professional women live and work in New York. TV series.

Mad about You. A married couple deal with life in the nineties. TV series.

On Becoming a Doctor. Medical school students are followed throughout their classroom and clinical experience at Harvard. PBS documentary.

The Paper Chase. First-year law students encounter the pressures of preparing to be lawyers. Video.

The Real World. MTV series brings together groups of young people, provides a place for them to live, and records what happens.

Reality Bites. New graduates experience life after college. Video.

Ruby in Paradise. A young woman leaves her Tennessee home and heads to Florida to try to make a life on her own. Video.

Single White Female. A young career woman in New York City unknowingly agrees to share her apartment with the roommate from hell. Video.

Singles. Twentysomethings try to find themselves, and one another, in Seattle. Video.

St. Elmo's Fire. A group of Georgetown University graduates struggle during their first year out. Video.

Uncommon Women and Others. A group of college graduates reunite and remember their senior year at Mount Holyoke. Play by Wendy Wasserstein.

Wall Street. A young man anxious to make it big in the financial world gets corrupted into doing it the dishonest way. Video.

With Honors. Several Harvard seniors learn about life, compassion, and what honor really means through their relationship with a homeless man. Video.

INDEX

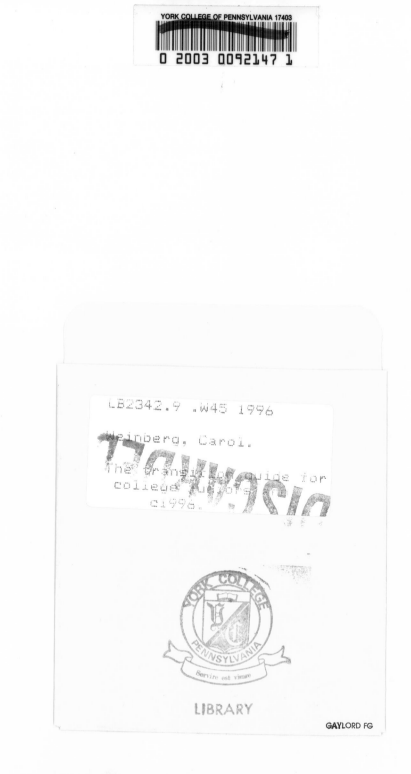